KEYS TO REVELATION:

MESSAGES IN:

- LETTERS

- SYMBOLS, AND

- PATTERNS

DONALD R. MIESNER

DEDICATION TO:

Otto and Ella, my parents, and my nine siblings, for life and nurture in the family of the faithful;

Wilma, my wife, and Lori, Judy, and Ami, our children, for love and companionship along life's way;

My colleagues and professors in the Concordia system of colleges and seminaries, for their stimulation and friendship;

My Concordia/New York students for the shared walk through the labyrinthian paths of the apocalypse; and

John Springer, for skillful assistance in the final formatting of this book.

TABLE OF CONTENTS

beast from the land), inflict great deprivation and suffering on the faithful. A call for endurance. The mark of the beast (666) identifies it for what it is!

The bliss of the 144,000 on Mt. Zion. Three urgent messages. The second call for endurance. Three voices from heaven. These 144,000 were earlier sealed. They symbolize all the redeemed of all ages. It is a numberless throng that praises God and the Lamb. Two paradoxes pave the path to paradise. Other scenes of hope in Revelation.

Revelation 20 highlights the enthronement and reign with Christ. Satan's binding and loosing frame the millennium. The redeemed are blessed by sharing in the first resurrection; the second death cannot hold them. The final showdown, generally perceived as Armageddon, is ushered in by the millennium. It is mirrored in three ways. Rev. 16 displays the crushing of the demonic forces by the power of the Almighty. Rev. 19 presents the victorious redeemer riding forth with the armies of heaven annihilating His foes. Rev. 20 shows Satan defeated at the beloved city and consigned with his henchmen to the lake of fire. Those named in the book of life receive everlasting blessedness at the great white throne.

A tale of two cities: Babylon falls and New Jerusalem dramatically appears. Babylon's portrait as "sin city" is sketched from ancient origins to apostolic times, where her identity is fused with that of Rome. New Jerusalem stands in sharp contrast with both historic Jerusalem and Babylon. Former evils are "no more," and numerous reasons for limitless joy are portrayed. The chapter begins with suggested Bible readings, and ends with questions for study and reflection; this is similar to the format of chapter nine.

A tale of two women: one faithful and true; the other depraved and destructive. They are of opposite purposes. The goodly woman (the bride) is depicted as: with endangered child; preserved amid persecution; bride of the Lamb; and New Jerusalem itself!

Conversely, the harlot is: in cahoots with the scarlet beast, royally robed, completely corrupt, drunk with the blood of the martyrs, situated on "the seven hills," is "the great city," and doomed to defeat with the seven kings.

Seven is John's favorite digit. It shapes the outline of the book and its seven-fold cycle of messages of hope. The seven letters, seals, trumpets, signs, bowls, and sights give structure and movement to the cyclical, ever-developing, visions of John. The beatitudes, scattered throughout the book, are a seventh seven that integrates the theology of the apocalypse.

AUTHOR'S PREFACE

For many years Revelation was a book of mystery to me until I more seriously took its challenge: "Blessed is he who reads aloud the words of prophecy, and blessed are those who hear, and who keep what is written therein; for the time is near." (Rev. 1:3)

It happened in 1974 when I began to teach a New Testament survey course at Concordia College in Bronxville, NY. While a survey can easily skim the surface of parts of a longer anthology, that approach seemed inadequate to me. I needed to make this last book of the Bible my very own also. Deeper and comprehensive study soon led to my teaching Revelation as a separate regular college course. As I came to understand St. Jerome's observation of Revelation as "the holy of holies" of the Bible, I was invited to do workshops and Bible classes on Revelation in churches of our tri-state service area (NY, CT, and NJ), as well as extension school courses in MD and FL. More recently, I was privileged to teach Bible classes on the Apocalypse also in my current home state of MO.

Now, as a return gift to the church, which passed on to me the comforting and hope-filled message of the gospel of Jesus Christ, I wish to reinvest a part of this legacy with others. Hopefully, they may be inspired, as I have been, to cling to the life-giving hope delivered long ago to the people of God who sought a sure compass for life's journey in troubled times.

Keys to Revelation is not a verse by verse commentary like some of the fine works listed in my bibliography. Rather, its approach is to supplement them with fresh insights and by further lifting the veil of esoteric language and the remote first century historic and cultural context. The focus here will be on Revelation's primary themes as clarified through the use of John's literary tools of symbols, patterns, and letters as keys to understanding. Hopefully, this will aid the reader in decoding and applying the encouraging message of "hope for today, courage for tomorrow." That hope is based on God's unfailing promises, revealed for the persevering saints "whose robes have been washed in the blood of the Lamb" (Rev. 7:14).

FOREWORD

This present volume entitled *Keys to Revelation* is a well thought out and in-depth presentation of the symbolic language that the author of Revelation uses to present the message and truths of the last book of the Bible.

The author, Donald R. Miesner, presents and defines the various symbols, numbers, pictures, etc. to help the reader of Revelation to receive and understand faithfully the message of Revelation.

As one reads Revelation and uses this well-written "Keys to Revelation" as a guide to understanding its written style, this last book of the Bible will become linguistically meaningful to the reader.

This writing of Dr. Miesner is not a commentary of Revelation, but rather an introduction to the use of a commentary.

Louis A. Brighton

INTRODUCTION

Revelation is a book rich in gospel for all ages. Yet, for many, Revelation is a closed book because of its symbolic language. For those who insist on interpreting it literally, it seems bizarre. However, for John's original audience, its symbols were understood for their comfort and encouragement. The book has continuing relevance for those who heed the opening beatitude (Rev. 1:3) and see the rich message that leaps out of its unique historic and cultural context.

The people of God endured severe persecution in the centuries surrounding the birth of Christ. The persecution in the second century B.C. by Antiochus Epiphanes led to the slaughter of many Jews and the desecration of Jerusalem's temple. For the faithful survivors, the veiled language of apocalyptic became a useful tool for inspiring courage in the oppressed people of God. This form of picture language was understood by "the people of the book" but was incomprehensible to their secular opponents. When in John's time the churches of Asia were subject to violence and discrimination, this literary form again proved useful. It makes heavy use of the symbolism of numbers and allusions to the imagery of the Old Testament, as well as to the redemptive work of Jesus.

John issued the call for perseverance to the churches from exile on the isle of Patmos. He reminded them that God is King of kings and Lord of lords. Contemporary political forces of intimidation and terror would ultimately fall before Him. The faithful would receive everlasting blessedness at the hand of the Almighty. In John's day the persecutions came from the Roman emperors' decrees. In later ages persecutions would arise from various secular authorities who demand allegiance to ways that would remove God from the center of life.

In keeping with the style of apocalypse, the themes of Revelation show the stark contrast of good versus evil, God versus Satan, and monotheism versus polytheism. Also, the focus is highly eschatological. God will reward His own in ways that make present adversity seem trifling. He has the last word. In the final judgment the anti-Christian oppressor will be doomed while the saints will receive everlasting blessedness in heaven. Worship of the Father and the Lamb is a dominant theme throughout Revelation. It emanates from the angels, from the faithful of all ages, and from all of creation. By contrast, worship of the emperor is compromised at best in its polytheistic setting, and is bankrupt in its quality, even if forcefully applied.

While the literary style of the book poses challenges, even the casual reader of Revelation can pick out its dominant themes. These include the sovereignty of God, the opposition of Satan and his supporters against the church, the call to the suffering saints for patient endurance, Christ's victorious return to judge the wicked and to reward the righteous, the final devastation of Satan and his followers, and the eternal blessedness of the people of God.

Revelation is not a chronological blueprint for church history as some interpreters would have it. Rather, its pattern of the visions of the 7 seals, 7 trumpets, and 7 bowls is cyclical in nature, covering the same time frame, the period of the church, each with increasing intensity. John guides the apocalypse to a climax, using the pattern of clashing symbols of two cities (Babylon and New Jerusalem) and two women (the Bride and Harlot Babylon).

In its opening chapters and in its final verse, the book takes on a letter form. It offers instruction in living out the will of God in daily life, as well as consistently reminding the reader of God's gracious reward for their fidelity. Despite the adversity encountered in life, He stands by them to the end. Not all of God's ways will always be understood in time. That's why the call to endurance and the glorious interludes of the book are so pivotal.

To read Revelation with understanding requires a readiness to see the major theological themes that are couched in a literary style difficult for most modern readers. When symbolic details are forced into a literalistic mode, for example in regard to the thousand years, meaning is easily distorted. However, for those willing to explore and apply the historic and literary context of John's people, the reward for faith and life is priceless.

CHAPTER I

GETTING INTO REVELATION

Many devout Christians over the centuries agreed with Martin
Luther's early assessment of the book of Revelation when he stated,

> "They are supposed to be blessed who keep what is written in
> this book; and yet no one knows what that is, to say nothing of
> keeping it. This is just the same as if we did not have the book
> at all."[1]

Fortunately, Luther's later studies led him to reflect in 1546, "We can
profit from this book and make good use of it. First for our comfort; .
. . second, for our warning."[2] Within the last generation in particular
many excellent works have appeared that lift the veil of mystery from
Revelation. The path to being able to read, hear, and heed its
liberating and sustaining gospel message is now open.

Regrettably, however, there remains a genre of sensationalistic
books that misrepresent such concepts as the "rapture" of the saints,
the "tribulation" which the church endures as she enters the kingdom
of God (Acts 14:22), the "millennium,"[3] and a host of other points.
Our treatment will focus on the positive use that John gives these
concepts and in a way fully consistent with the wider spectrum of the
witness of the Bible. For example, the New Testament refers to only
one return of Jesus to earth. That will be at the end of time, when He
will separate the sheep from the goats (Matt. 24:36-44; 25:31-32).
Accordingly, the sensationalistic views which fall short of credible
support in the sacred Scriptures will be sublimated.

Before getting too deeply into the themes, symbols, and patterns of
the book, it is well to examine the who, why, when, where, and how of
it. Who was John? Why did he write? When and where did it
happen? How could he succeed in communicating while using such
seemingly esoteric literary devices?

WHO? The author simply describes himself as John. Apparently,
there was no need to identify himself further to his addressees, the
churches of Asia. It is transparent in John's seven letters to the

churches that he has intimate knowledge both of their local history and culture and of their spiritual condition and need. Such knowledge can best be explained as that of one whom earliest tradition identifies as John, son of Zebedee, the Beloved Disciple. This John was known to have served as bishop of Ephesus toward the end of the first century and at the close of the apostolic age.[4]

WHY was the book written? John, finding himself in exile because of "the word of God and the testimony of Jesus" (Rev. 1:9), felt the need to strengthen the faithful people of the churches of Asia. The letters to the churches was his best chance of rendering his pastoral and spiritual support. The faith of the churches was endangered by false teachers and by the loss of spiritual fervor from within. From the outside, they were slandered and opposed by Jews and persecuted by the enforcers of emperor worship. Some had lost their lives, and John, their spiritual leader, had been banished. John's purpose, then, is one of giving comfort and encouragement to the faithful and of warning to the straying and lost. Specifically, he wrote:

- to encourage fidelity to Jesus by pointing to the triumph and the promises of the risen Christ;
- to reveal Christ as the only one worthy and able to insure a glorious future;
- to show that emperor worship and polytheism are counterfeit and forms of satanic opposition to God;
- to call to spiritual renewal and/or repentance all who would read, hear, and heed the gospel call; and
- to warn persecutors and backsliders by portraying the dreadful consequence of denying, defying, or opposing God and His people.

WHEN? Even though occasional persecutions occurred before the time of Emperor Domitian, such as Nero's massacre of Christians at Rome in the sixties, which claimed the lives of Peter, Paul, and others, emperor worship was not widely enforced until the nineties of the first century. Then Christians became especially vulnerable. In some cases, they were exposed to authorities by Jews who felt threatened by the new faith in the resurrected Lord which was gaining adherents from the synagog ranks. It was at this time that John was exiled to the isle of Patmos in the Aegean Sea. At a later date Polycarp, bishop of Smyrna, would be slain for his insistence on worshiping only the Christian God, and not the emperor.[5]

Already in the earliest days of the empire, Rome had felt the need to cement the loyalty of the diverse tribes and nations that they had conquered along the shores of the Mediterranean Sea. The worship of the goddess Roma was promoted at first. But, to worship an idea or a spirit was perceived to be ineffective in promoting the desired loyalty. So, they deified the emperors from Octavian (Augustus) onward in order to obtain a more personal effect. In time, all people, regardless of their other religious ties, were asked to offer once a year the ritual incense and to proclaim the emperor as "Lord and God" (*Dominus et Deus*). This seems to have brought on the crisis of faith that John addressed from exile in Patmos during Domitian's reign. The time is likely around 95 A.D., as indicated by the early church historian, Eusebius.

WHERE? John wrote from exile on the island of Patmos, located in the Aegean Sea, sixty five miles southwest of Ephesus. The seven churches he addressed are situated in cities of the province of Asia, which is in the westernmost region of modern Turkey. These cities were centers of worship of both the emperor and of Greco-Roman deities. Co-existence amid such religious diversity made the churches particularly vulnerable. More will be said about the uniqueness of these cities in the chapter on the seven churches.

HOW John chose to communicate was practical, inspirational, and puzzling at the same time, depending on the readership. While it would have puzzled and perhaps even amused the Roman enforcers, who may have viewed John's scroll at a check point, as product of a writer's mind gone wild, it would be readily understood by the people of the churches of Asia, who could "crack the code." John's use of images and symbols from the Old Testament would relate meaningfully to his faithful flock which was at home in the Scriptures. It would be meaningless and confusing to outsiders who might intercept and destroy John's message if they understood its content.

After all, John did give courage and hope to his intended readers by pointing to the eventual downfall of their persecutors as the forces of Satan.

Victory, he assured them, would come to the faithful when the Lord returned, as promised, to reward the persevering saints. The glories of the New Jerusalem (heaven) would be wondrous for them beyond human imagination, even as the demise of the oppressive Babylon (Rome) would be terrifying to her supporters. Thus, John was both practical and wise in using apocalyptic language, replete with Biblical images and symbols that were part of the Hebrew heritage of the churches. These symbols, in turn, were largely incomprehensible to those who would collaborate with the enforcers of the Roman imperial decretals, that gave great grief and suffering to Christians who were determined to remain "faithful unto death."

APOCALYPTIC STYLE

John refers to his "book" as an "apocalypse" (1:1). Apocalyptic writing was a common form of expression among God's people in the three centuries that stretched from about 200 B.C. to 100 A.D. This was a time of intense persecution of the faithful that began with the Seleucid dynasty of the Syrians and resurfaced from time to time, and especially in Emperor Domitian's reign. Among the severest persecutions were those that occurred at the time of the desecration of the temple in Jerusalem in 167 B.C. by Antiochus IV. Nearly three centuries later John found himself exiled on Patmos during the Roman attempt to extinguish the life of the church in Asia.

This style of writing is characterized by the hope it could give to the oppressed saints through coded language. It would be understood by those who owned and knew the symbols, but was meaningless to outsiders and, importantly so, to the enemy. The hope, conveyed in such writings, usually involved the defeat of the oppressor. Of necessity, such a message needed to be camouflaged in order to avoid dire consequences for both the writer and the intended readers. That the message penetrated enemy defenses was critical "for the consolation of the saints."

The style of apocalypse is characterized by two predominant elements: dualism and eschatology. The dualism reflects sharp contrasts, for example good vs. evil; God vs. Satan; Michael and his angelic corps vs. the evil angels; light vs. darkness; rewards and punishments, etc. Eschatology focuses on end-time matters such as death, resurrection, and the life of the world to come. It has its culmination in the return of the Messiah to make all things new and right.

Secondary characteristics of apocalypse include the use of vision; a messiah figure who opposes the antichrist; pseudonymity; predicted woes; animal symbolism; and numerology.[6] Most of these aspects are found in Revelation. Yet, John is not slavishly adherent to all these points. He freely identifies himself as the writer. It is important that the churches of Asia recognize that the message is from their faithful and credible spiritual shepherd. Likewise, the church of later ages benefits from the same knowledge, shared by the "Beloved Disciple," who intimately knew the mind of Jesus.

PRINCIPLES OF INTERPRETATION

The symbolic language of Revelation prevents many from reading it and benefiting from its uplifting message. It confuses others who do read it. Generally accepted principles of interpretation need to be kept in mind as one attempts to "hear and keep" the message of "the Revelation of Jesus Christ."

1. *Every important doctrine of Scripture is taught clearly somewhere in the Bible in plain literal language.* Revelation introduces no novel doctrines. It does accentuate many key doctrines presented previously in Scripture.

2. *Imagery is used in various books of the Bible.* This is especially true of several prophetic Old Testament books. Even Jesus

used metaphorical language when He called Herod a fox and said that Christians are salt and light. Revelation carries the use of symbols to a new level.

3. *Symbolic language does convey meaning for those who understand the symbols.* The churches of Asia knew the imagery of the Old Testament that John used. Even Jesus spoke in veiled language when He instructed in parables. His disciples understood; His opponents were kept "in the dark" thereby.

4. *Scripture interprets Scripture.* Clear passages elsewhere shed light on difficult and novel expressions in Revelation. The early church rigidly excluded from her collection of inspired Scripture (the canon) any and all writings that were not totally in doctrinal agreement.

5. *The visions of Revelation are cyclical in nature.* As John progresses with the series of seven seals, trumpets, and bowls, the time frame is always the same: the age of the church. It stretches from Jesus' first coming to His second (and final!) coming. Each cycle, however, increases in intensity and with fresh insights, as it progresses toward the book's (and the church's) consummation. The succession of cycles does **not** prophesy a succession of periods of world history, as some past interpreters supposed.

6. *Not every detail is significant in itself.* As with the parables of Jesus, details are sometimes merely the framework for a single point. The reader need not feel overly frustrated by an obscure detail. There is no shame in admitting, "I don't know." John's churches understood more than we can. They were not a score of centuries or thousands of miles removed from the events before them. The composite message of Revelation is clear and simple once we apply the meaning of the known symbols; it is well worth the effort of such "reading, hearing, and keeping."

7. *The language of apocalypse is generously used by John.* The above section on "apocalypticism" explains its need and practical value for the churches of Asia at the time of John.

PRIMARY DOCTRINES

The chief teachings of the Apocalypse are geared to the needs of the church of Asia in John's time. They serve to inspire Christians of all ages also, especially those who crave "courage for today and hope for tomorrow" as they persevere in the midst of life's tribulations. The main foci of Revelation include those that follow.

1. *Christ is present with the church and cares for her.* He holds the seven stars in His hand (1:13, 16). The Bride joins the Lamb in marriage (19:7-9). In heaven the faithful will bask in the delight of the intimate presence of the Father and the Lamb.

2. *The wicked will be judged severely.* This is a repeated message in the seven-fold series of seals, trumpets, and bowls as well as in the final demise of Babylon and her adherents, the beast and the false prophet, and the dragon (Satan!) too.

3. *Christians too will be accountable for fidelity to Christ.* The messages to the seven churches warns against being unwatchful, backsliding, and straying.

4. *God is transcendent.* He has no equals outside of Himself. The Lamb is enthroned as equal and as one with the Father.

5. *God is in complete control of nature and human destiny.* Those who don't do His bidding will eventually pay the penalty. The faithful flock (the sealed of Rev. 7) will not be tempted beyond their ability to stand. Those whose names are in the book of life (the redeemed) can depend on the salvation He has secured through Jesus.

6. *Satan's power is limited.* He cannot exceed what God tolerates during the short time (12:12) he has left.

7. *Hell is a place for punishment.* It is reserved for evil spirits, human transgressors, and for all that is evil.

8. *The reward for the just is a glorious one.* The resurrection life is one of unlimited and perpetual peace and joy. Heaven is described in terms of magnificence, beyond the limits of present human experience.

9. *The Christian's hope for eternity is well grounded.* The Lamb has ransomed men for God; and God is love! (1 John 4:8)

10. *Until the Lord returns, God's people will live amid suffering.* "In the world you will have tribulation," Jesus said, "but be of good cheer, I have overcome the world" (John 16:33).

It has been said that the book of Revelation is "crammed with heaven, but only those who see take off their shoes."[7] It is our prayer that your study will enable the assurance that in Revelation's pages is found the holy ground of God's sure and glorious promises.

THE INTRODUCTORY CHAPTER

In subsequent chapters we will focus on primary themes and literary devices, including symbols and patterns, that convey the message of Revelation. To give direction to these foci, we will use John's opening chapter to introduce the basic content that follows, as did John in writing his book.

John begins by stating his primary intent, that of revealing Jesus Christ (1:1). The first of John's seven beatitudes (1:3) shows both the benefit and the urgency of this message. The churches get a Trinitarian greeting (vv. 4-5) culminating in Jesus as witness, firstborn, and ruler. Thus, there is stressed, in succession, His fidelity, His conquest of death, and His dominion over all rulers. All glory is owed to Him who is our lover, our liberator and our enabler (vv. 5-6). He will return on a cloud, even as he had ascended; and all will see Him, even His enemies (all tribes of the earth) to their grief! (v. 7)

John is on the isle of Patmos suffering for the faith, yet not silenced! His message is for the universal church, as reflected through the seven named churches of Asia (vv. 9-11).

John shared his vision of the exalted Christ (vv. 12-16) as one who is in the midst of the churches (v. 12, the lampstands, bearers of "the Light of the world," John 8:12; 9:5). He is her high priest (v. 13, wearing a robe with a golden girdle); He is with dignity and purity (His head and hair are white as wool and snow); is omniscient (eyes penetrating like a flame of fire); and with all power (strong feet), authority and dominion (strong voice, 2-edged sword). He holds His messengers to the churches (the seven stars, or angels) in His protective right hand (vv. 16, 20). "Christ's face and person radiate God's glory, which brings light to a world of darkness."[8] (v. 16)

Although John is at first stunned with fear at the vision of Jesus, he is quickly reassured by "the ruler of kings" (v. 5). The one who conquered death and is "alive forevermore" renews John's strength and empowers him to write to the churches (vv. 17-19) with "the words of eternal life." (John 6:68)

---

[1]Luther, Martin. Prefaces to the New Testament. Translated by Charles M. Jacobs. Revised by Theodore Bachmann. Reprint of Fortress publication. St. Louis: Concordia Publishing House, 1972, p. 48.

[2]Ibid., p. 54.

[3]The period between the "binding" and "loosing" of Satan is generally understood by mainline Christian scholars as the "elastic" time frame between Jesus' victorious resurrection and ascension to heaven and His return on Judgment Day.

[4]The view that it may have been a different John was first suggested in the third century A.D., most notably by bishop Dionysius of Alexandria. Even though this view has many modern adherents, the evidence from the early church strongly supports authorship by John, the apostle. For more discussion, see Louis Brighton's commentary, <u>Revelation</u>. Concordia Commentary. St. Louis: Concordia Publishing House, 1999, pages 12-15.

[5] "The Martyrdom of the Holy Polycarp, Bishop of Smyrna," <u>The Apostolic Fathers: An American Translation</u> by Edgar J. Goodspeed. New York: Harper & Brothers, 1950, pages 245-256.

[6] Rist, M. "Apocalypticism," <u>The Interpreter's Dictionary of the Bible.</u> Volume I. New York: Abingdon Press, 1962, pages 157-161.

[7] Richardson, Donald. <u>The Revelation of Jesus Christ.</u> Paperback. Atlanta: John Knox Press, 1976, page 13.

[8] Brighton, Louis. <u>Revelation.</u> page 51.

CHAPTER II

SYMBOLISM

Revelation has a common bond with other apocalyptic literature of the several centuries immediately preceding and succeeding the age of Jesus. This is true especially in its use of the symbolism of numbers and other imagery found throughout the Old Testament and in intertestamental literature.

John, of necessity, chooses to communicate with his people through such symbols with which they are familiar from the writings and the thought world of the Hebrews. The imagery serves a critical purpose, that of shielding the meaning of his politically sensitive message from those who represent the imperial power structure (their persecutors); the latter cannot decode the symbolism or understand the imagery. In this way John is able from exile to get the message past his adversaries to the persevering saints for their encouragement in the promises of Jesus.

There are many references to the O.T. in Revelation. Metzger (Breaking the Code, p. 13) points out that 278 verses of the 404 found in Revelation's 22 chapters contain one or more O.T. allusions. Jenkins (The Old Testament in the Book of Revelation, pp. 23-24) refers to Tenney's identification of 348 such allusions, 95 of them repeated, for a total of 253 different passages referenced.

Because of John's frequent use of the symbolism of numbers and their application, a separate chapter will be devoted to decode their significance.

In our survey of the N.T. Apocalypse, our focus here will be to ferret out most of the most significant images that have an impact on the meaning of the book's message. Where appropriate, applications of the meaning will be offered. For those O.T. allusions made by John which are not developed here, a comprehensive commentary on Revelation will be useful, such as those by Brighton, Hendriksen, and Mounce. An examination of prominent images follows.

(Rev. 1:3) blessed. This word introduces the first of the seven "beatitudes" of Revelation. Other listings are at Rev. 14:13; 16:15; 19:9; 20:6; and 22:7, 14. Taken together, they frame and pinpoint the eschatological hope of the book.

(1:4) throne: the seat of Him whose is the kingdom, the power, and the glory. Though adversaries lay false claim to godly thrones, there is only one who reigns supreme over all; He is King of kings and Lord of lords (19:1-6, 16).

(1:7; 14:6) tribes of the earth. Those who wail at Jesus' return on the clouds refer to the non-Christian world, those who have reason to dread the judgment because of their impenitence. See also 9:4; 16:1-2, 9, 11, 21 and Matthew 24:30. (Obviously, the people of faith will welcome Christ's return with joy. Note: the fervent prayer of the closing chapter of Revelation that He come soon!)

(1:9) tribulation. This refers to the suffering or deprivation of those who are faithful to Christ. Thus, in John 16:33 Jesus alerts His followers to the reality that "in the world you will have tribulation"; and Paul stated that "through many tribulations we must enter the kingdom of God" (Acts 14:22). The church of Smyrna would have "ten days" of tribulation (a brief time, 2:10). Nowhere else does John assign a fixed time frame to the concept of tribulation. Those who create a literal 7 year period of tribulation here (using Daniel as their reference point) do violence to the symbolic usage of "seven" common to both Revelation and the apocalyptic sections of Daniel.

(1:8 Alpha and Omega. The first and last letters of the Greek alphabet suggest Jesus as "the beginning and the end," the Sovereign Lord of all that takes place from the creation to the consummation, and even includes all eternity. This concept is reaffirmed in 21:6 and 22:13.

(1:12) lampstands. These refer to the churches of Asia (as 1:20 explains!). The usual function of lampstands is to support lamps, which in turn give light to the surrounding area. The imagery hints at Jesus' self-disclosure as "Light of the world" (John 8:12; 9:5).

(1:16) two-edged sword. The sword in Christ's mouth is the word of judgment, which is even more to be respected and feared than the *ius gladii*, the right to execute granted the proconsul at Pergamum (2:12).

(1:18) Death and Hades. The two are always closely related in Revelation (6:8; 20:13-14). Hades is the place of the dead (e.g., the grave).

(#2 and 3) Symbolic terms from these chapters will be dealt with in the chapter on the seven churches.

(4:4 *et al.*) 24 elders. They represent the saints of all time (the 12 tribes and 12 apostles represent the faithful of O.T. and N.T. ages).

(4:6 *et al.*) 4 living creatures. They symbolize God's animate creation in its worship around the throne.

(5:1 *et al.*) scroll. It is God's "book" containing mankind's future.

(5:5) The Lion of the tribe of Judah, the Root of David. These two pictures refer to the Lamb (mentioned in 5:6). Both refer to O.T. passages seen as messianic in the first century. Judah, the "lion's whelp" (of Gen. 49:9-10) is a direct patriarchal ancestor of Christ; and Isaiah 11:1 foreshadows the ideal king of the line of David, "the shoot from the stump of Jesse."

(5:6) Lamb. The designation most frequently given to Jesus throughout Revelation, it draws on the symbolism of John 1:29, 36 where the Baptist identifies Jesus as "the Lamb of God." He is the perfect atoning sacrifice.

(5:9) new song. It praises God in that the promises of the O.T. now have their fulfillment in the redeeming life of the Lamb, whose blood ransomed men for God. See also 14:3 and 15:3-4 regarding this song.

(6:2) white horse. The horse represents conquest. The rider of this horse differs from the rider of 19:11, where Christ rides forth triumphantly with His heavenly retinue in conquest of His enemies. The rider in 6:2 is in parallel with the three others that follow, all of whom symbolize destruction, destitution, and devastation of various kinds. The rider in 6:2 is a parody of the one in 19:11. (Similarly, the beast from the earth of 13:11 deceptively assumes a Lamb-like quality.)

(6:10) "How long?" This *question* reflects the yearning of the Lord's people for His return to "restore" righteousness and peace. Its *answer* is at the heart of the book's purpose: to reassure the faithful.

(6:10) those who dwell on the earth. Throughout Revelation this phrase refers to those who persecute and oppress the people of God. This group includes idolaters, murderers and other evildoers who are unwilling to repent. They reject the messiahship of Jesus and the witness of His adherents. For similar references, see Rev. 8:13; 11:10; 14:6; and 17:2, 8.

(6:11) white robe: the garment that signals the blessedness of the faithful who have received "the crown of life." See also 3:4-5, 18; 4:4; 7:9, 13; and 19:14.

(7:1) four angels, corners, winds. The four winds refer to destructive agents. God's guardian angels are depicted as protecting the saints (the 144,000) throughout the entire earth (the metaphorical four corners) from destruction (of the four winds). The saints are sealed (protected) from the Evil One for salvation, assuming their perseverance in faith and hope in the Savior.

(7:4, 9) every tribe of Israel. These are the redeemed, those who have received cleansing in the blood of the Lamb. These tribes are carefully distinguished from "the tribes *of the earth*," referred to as those who oppose or fail to follow the Lamb (cf. Rev. 1:7 and Matt. 24:30).

(7:5-8) the absence of Dan and Ephraim. These two tribes, which received lands in the allotments at Joshua's time are not here named. Instead, Levi and Joseph are listed to complete the twelve. The context of Revelation is consistent in referring to God's people as inclusive of those who are faithful to Him. Thus, it is not surprising that the fluid number of the 12 tribes deletes the names of the two tribes that housed the idolatrous O.T. shrines at Dan and Bethel (the latter in Ephraim's territory). Here Joseph (father of Ephraim, who

23

was allotted lands) is named with his other son Manasseh. Also, Levi, the priestly tribe (without lands) is a convenient fill-in for Dan.

(7:9) a great multitude: the countless throng which has been faithful unto death and rejoices in its salvation before the throne of God and the Lamb. In 19:6 this multitude sounds forth its "hallelujahs."

(7:14) white in the blood: a mixed metaphor indicating (not color but) righteousness and purity (symbolized by "white"). Thus, the "red" blood of the Lamb has made the robes of the redeemed "white."

(7:17) the Lamb as shepherd. Jesus, the Lamb of God, is the Good Shepherd of John 10 as well as the fulfillment of Psalm 23. He safely guides His own through "the valley of the shadow of death."

(8:2 et al.) trumpets. These instruments are used generally in Scripture, as in Revelation, to announce or to initiate important events. Here they introduce God's judgmental visitations. Elsewhere they signal the Lord's return (e.g., Matt. 24:31; 1 Cor. 15:52; 1 Thess. 4:16).

(8:11) Wormwood. The name of the "fallen star" signifies a bitter polluting poison. It recalls the poisoned waters that idolatrous Israel would drink as penalty for her infidelities (Jeremiah 9:15 and 23:15).

(8:13; 14:6) mid-heaven: a lofty location where the eagle could be seen and heard by all as it announces judgment to "the dwellers of the earth."

(9:1-2, 11; 11:7; 20:1, 3) the bottomless pit: the abode of Satan and his agents of deceit and destruction.

(9:11) Abaddon and Apollyon. Both names mean "Destroyer." This aptly describes "the king of the bottomless pit." See also Job 26:6; 28:22; Ps. 88:11; and Prov. 15:11.

(9:14; 16:12) the Euphrates River: the eastern boundary of the Roman Empire. Rome's fear of the enemy that lurked beyond this border is given eschatological meaning by John, signaling the onset of judgment on the wicked.

(10:1; 14:14ff.) cloud: either the visible means indicating presence, or the vehicle of transportation between heaven and earth for God's messenger. Similarly, the N.T. portrays Jesus as received into heaven by a cloud and returning for judgment at the end of the age.

(10:3-4) seven thunders. This symbolizes the majestic roar of the Lord's voice. It is a likely allusion to Ps. 29 where "the voice of the Lord" sounds forth mightily seven times upon His created world.

(11:3) two witnesses. Two is the number of witness and of support. The identity of the two in chapter 11 is a fluid one, passing quickly from portrayal of Joshua and Zerubbabel to that of Moses and Elijah. The message is clear. God stands by His witnesses, whoever they are, as they represent Him and suffer for the faith. Their final reward is the summons to the glory of heaven (11:4-12).

(11:8) the great city, allegorically called Sodom and Egypt. Two historic havens of harlotry (Sodom) and oppression (Egypt) are fused to depict "the great city" (Jerusalem), which was no longer "the holy city." The wickedness of Jerusalem's crucifiers in John's time had overtaken Babylon/Rome and would be perpetuated in whatever city would foster independence of the Creator and oppression of His creatures. For further references to "the great city," see Rev. 17:18 and 18:16.

(12:1,3; 15:1) sign. Thrice here the word "sign" points to a significant eschatological scene. Elsewhere (Rev. 13:13f.; 16:14; 19:20) the word alludes to deceptive Satanic actions. The 7-fold appearance of signs in Revelation calls to mind the seven signs (and the seven great "I am's") of John's Gospel, which reflect on Jesus' eschatological action.

(12:3) the dragon. This is the common portraiture of Satan throughout the rest of the book. See especially 12:9.

(12:4; 13:1; 17:3) heads, horns, diadems: here identify the Satanic forces and reflect the devil's power (horns), throne (diadems), and authority (heads). See 13:2b for these identifications. This portraiture suggests, in triplicate, a dominant and mighty force such as that embodied in Rome's power structure of Emperor Domitian's time.

(12:5) rod of iron. Ps. 2:9 presents this instrument as the means of triumphing and ruling over the enemy. Here (and in 2:27 and 19:15) it is applied to the victorious Messiah who leads the faithful to their ultimate reward: triumph over Satan and his cohorts.

(13:16f.) mark. Those identifying with the beast's idolatrous purposes are seen as bearing its mark. The terrible fate of those so aligned is noted in 14:9-11. This is in sharp contrast with the lot of those who bear the name of the Lamb and the Father (14:1-5).

(14:4) virgins: the symbol of spiritual fidelity. Those on Mount Zion (in God's presence) who sing the joyous "new song" of redemption have not given in to the "lie" (14:5) of declaring the emperor to be "Lord and God." Thus, they "have not defiled themselves with women (the idolatrous liaison with "the harlot Babylon"). They differ from those in the fold of "Babylon," with whom the idolaters had committed spiritual fornication (17:1-6).

(14:8) Babylon. This name, appearing first here in Revelation, recurs in 16:19; 17:5; and 18:2, 10, 21. John uses the term to refer to the imperial and religious opponents and persecutors of the followers of Jesus Christ.

(14:20). blood: the issue from "the grapes of wrath," trodden out in the winepress of God's judgment on His sinful opponents. For background on this image of judgment, see Isaiah 63:1-6 and Joel 3:12-13.

(14:20) horse's bridle. The mention of the horse, immersed up to its bridle, draws attention to the implied rider (see 19:11-13), who rides forth victoriously over the satanic opponents at the final conquest. The robe of the rider is "dipped in blood," an apparent reference to the One who "trod the winepress" (on His horse)!

(15:5ff.) the temple of the tent of witness in heaven. Nothing escapes God's watchful eye. As God was present among His people who wandered the exodus trail, so His heavenly presence is there also in support of the faithful saints; their constancy amid trial will be vindicated through God's righteous actions in "the plagues" that enact judgment on the evil opponents.

(16:7ff.) the altar cry. Rev. 6:9-10 had voiced the cry of theodicy by the saints beneath heaven's altar. Their erstwhile question of when God would finally work out judgment on the power-mongering persecutors is here answered in the portraiture of God's fearsome final outpouring of fury on "Babylon."

(16:16) Armageddon. Megiddo's mount (and city) was the preferred site for ancient battles in Israel (such as those in the times of Deborah and Barak and of King Josiah). Here it is used metaphorically to depict the final universal judgment of God's opponents (and the vindication of the righteous).

(17:1) harlot. Here Babylon is depicted as an agent of seduction. As Israel of O.T. times was led astray by a perverse fertility cult and later tested by ancient Babylon's religious system, so its first century surrogate (Rome) had enforced idolatrous worship upon its subjects. The utter demise of "harlot Babylon" perpetuates the prophetic judgment on those who go "a-whoring after other gods."

(17:2, 4) fornication. The worship of the emperor and other gods of the Roman pantheon is a type of spiritual adulteration (i.e., idolatry).

(17:9) wisdom. Even as "wisdom" was called for in 13:18 to identify the beast as part of an "unholy trinity" through the number 666, so John here locates the seat of power of the beast at the "seven hills," commonly understood as a reference to the city of Rome.

(17:12) one hour. The time of dominance of the perverse power structure hereby is denoted as brief and fleeting (in the context of eternity). Similarly, 18:10, 17, and 19 uses the same expression to indicate the swiftness with which God's judgment comes upon Babylon.

(18:16) purple and scarlet. The depiction of the opulent dress of "the great city" makes a clear connection with "the great harlot" of 17:1-4. She too was "arrayed in purple and scarlet." The city and the woman are "cut from the same cloth."

(19:1-6) hallelujah: mentioned four times in these verses, and only here in the N.T., it means "praise the Lord." It praises God's salvation and His judgments; it also exults in His reign and in the marriage of the Lamb to His Bride.

19:7) the Bride. The church (God's faithful people) is portrayed as the Bride of the Lamb (compare Eph. 5:23-32). The consummation of this blessed union is for those invited to "the marriage supper of the Lamb" (19:9). The lot of the faithful bride is a blessed one, opposite to that of "harlot Babylon," whose demise is lamented by her consorts (#18) and celebrated by those who survived her oppression (19:1-8).

(19:8,14) fine linen. The vesture of the Lamb's Bride, also that of "the armies of heaven," is the "righteous deeds of the saints." Similarly, Isaiah (in 61:10) praises God for covering him with "the robe of righteousness." This fine linen "bright and pure" (v. 8) or "white and pure" (v. 14) differs markedly from the fine linen of the doomed city, harlot Babylon, which was "purple and scarlet" (18:16; 17:4).

(19:20) the false prophet. This figure represents pseudo-religion, which attempts to have mankind worship powers opposed to Christ. His program of working "signs by which he deceived those who had received the mark of the beast" is detailed in 13:11-16 as that of "the beast from the earth"(another name for "the false prophet").

(19:20; 20:10) the lake of fire: hell, the repository of the beast, the false prophet, and the devil. Also, at the judgment, it is the fate of Death and Hades and of all those not recorded in the book of life (20:14f., 21:8).

(20:2) bound him . . . and threw him into the pit. The binding of Satan refers to the limitation placed on him by Christ through His death, resurrection and ascension. John 12:31 refers to the ruler of this world being "thrown out" in connection with Jesus' conquest of death. This was "the hour" by which Jesus glorified the Father and fulfilled His plan of salvation. Through these acts Jesus would "draw all men" to Himself (John 12:27-33). At the end of the "1000 years" Satan will be completely and finally thrown out (20:10). Through Jesus' resurrection, His steadfast followers are heirs of eternal life; and Satan cannot prevent that (John 10:30).

(20:3-7) the 1000 years. As elsewhere in Revelation, the number is to be taken symbolically. As explained in my chapter on the symbolism of numbers, 1000 (being the cube of 10) refers to utter completeness. Here the "1000 years" refers to the total time which elapses between Jesus' coming to earth to work out mankind's salvation (by which he "bound" Satan) and His return in glory to judge the world and to raise the saints to eternal blessedness. As Jesus said (Matt. 24:36), it will be in God's time, a date no man can foreknow.

(20:5-6) the rest of the dead. This includes those who were not His followers and who, thus, do not enjoy the presence and the glorious reign with Christ. They were and remain spiritually dead and, sadly, will eventually encounter the second death, the lake of fire, at the time of the final judgment (20:15; 21:8).

(20:5) the first resurrection/the second death. Those who died in the faith of Jesus "passed from death to life" (John 5:24) when they entered a living faith relationship with Jesus. That was their spiritual rebirth (or, "first" resurrection). At the time of their bodily resurrection, the "second death" (hell) will have no power over them. They reign with Christ already spiritually while they await His return to raise up and glorify their bodies for the enjoyment of the fullness of heavenly bliss. The "second death" will claim those who remained spiritually dead to God in their earthly life (20:14f.).

(20:8) Gog and Magog. Drawing on imagery from Ezekiel 38-39, John uses these two symbolic figures to represent the hostile nations of the world as playing a role in bringing on the end. Again, no specific geographic site is identified.

(20:9) the beloved city. Although one is tempted to identify this with Jerusalem, also called "the holy city" in Scripture, no sole location is singled out here; this is also true for the other final battle scenes of the book, namely Armageddon (16:16) and the battle waged between the armies of heaven and those of "the kings of the earth" (19:11-21). The "beloved city" is wherever (world-wide) God's people are. The forces of evil, deceived by the devil, will not prevail against them. The universal church of Christ will prevail, without casualty, saved by His intervention of grace!

(20:11) great white throne. See the earlier note on 1:4. Here the reference to a "great white" throne lends focus to the majesty and magnificence of the power and glory of the final Judge at the end of days. It recalls the eschatological words of Jesus found in Matthew 25:31-32.

(20:12-15; 21:27) the book of life: God's record of those who belong to Him, who carry the name of the Father and the Lamb. They are included in "New Jerusalem." The "dwellers on earth," who follow the beast, are excluded from this book (17:8).

(21:2) New Jerusalem. It is not the historic Jerusalem. Rather, it comes down out of heaven from God. It is presented as synonymous with the church, the Bride of the Lamb. It is the consummate holy city where God's presence with His people will abide forever. It is the city of God (21:10).

21:12, 14) the twelve tribes/apostles. New Jerusalem's gates and walls are inscribed with the names of the twelve tribes and twelve apostles, depicting the continuity between the leaders and saints of the O.T. and N.T. eras. Eph. 2:19-20 magnificently describes "the household of God" as "built upon the foundation of the apostles and prophets, Christ Jesus being Himself the cornerstone." Heaven will be populated with the heirs of the word proclaimed through the apostles and the prophets (and as also perpetuated through the twelve tribes).

(21:12ff.) gates: the points of entry to New Jerusalem, the court of the divine presence. God's messengers, twelve angels, are posted as greeters at heaven's gates, welcoming those who enter with the seal of the promise, transmitted through the twelve tribes.

(21: 15) measuring rod. Here the angel measures the holy city to assure John of its permanence. Even as the temple and the altar were to be measured by John in 11:1 to guarantee God's protection of the church on earth, so God confirms the perpetual security of the saints in heaven.

(21:22) temple. Old Jerusalem was seen as the holy city because of the temple, where God was seen to dwell in the midst of His people. Jesus deepened the definition of God's presence as He pointed to His own body through which God's visible presence on earth was manifest (John 2:19-22). Heaven's temple would not be a physical temple, constructed from stone. Rather, God's immanence would be manifest in His and the Lamb's glorious personal presence in the midst of the redeemed.

(21:23) lamp. The Lamb is New Jerusalem's "lamp." He is "the Light of the world" (John 8:12; 9:5) who dispels the world's darkness. The seven churches are the lampstands (1:20) where the lamp can beam forth His gospel rays and be the light of life for the world.

(22:2,19) the tree of life. Different from the tree in Eden's garden (Gen. 3:22-24), whose fruit fallen man was kept from eating, the tree of life in New Jerusalem is not only abundantly productive and available forever, but also therapeutic for the faithful. The promise made to the faithful of the church of Ephesus (2:7) comes to fruition in paradise.

(22:7) soon. The Lord's promise to return "soon" is to be seen in the context of God's time. As 2 Peter 3:8-9 reassures, "The Lord is not slow about His promise as some count slowness." Our thousand years to Him are as a day! Eternity is forever. In contrast, man's time on earth is short. In that sense, "the time is near" (1:3) when He will return for us. The urgency to live faithfully in man's fleeting years so that he may receive "the crown of (eternal) life" is heightened also in the letters to the churches (2:16; 3:11).

(22:7) coming. That is God's promise by which he encourages the faithful toward perseverance. That is also the prayer of the church with which the "revelation" closes. Seven times the verb for "coming" appears in the closing chapter (verses 7, 12, 17, and 20).

(22:15) dogs. The term is a metaphor for a wicked enemy, an evil-doer (Philippians 3:2).

(22:16) the bright morning star. The church of Thyatira (2:26-28) was promised the morning star for those who remain faithful to the end.

Here Jesus identifies Himself as that star. He is the promised star of Jacob (Numbers 24:17). His appearance signals the end of the church's long night of waiting for "the dayspring from on high" (Luke 1:78, KJV) to come. For that long-awaited appearance, the Spirit and the Bride fervently pray and say, "Come!" (22:17)

CHAPTER III

SIGNIFICANT NUMBERS

APOCALYPTIC USE

How numbers are interpreted in apocalyptic literature in general and in Revelation in particular separates mainline Christian interpretation of Revelation from that of dispensational thinkers on several critical points. In the two centuries immediately preceding and the one following the birth of Christ, Hebrew writers commonly employed numbers in their apocalyptic writings to convey spiritual or moral truth. Since numbers were used to express ideas, they were not meant to be read with literal exactness in apocalypse. Dispensational writers often disregard this principle and therefore come up with bizarre interpretations that are not in keeping with general Biblical truth. Thus, the Jehovah's Witnesses see heaven as populated by exactly 144,000. All others among the redeemed, they assert, would spend eternity in an earthly paradise, separate from those in heaven. Those who take the 1,000 years of Revelation 20 literally run into issues of dating the Lord's return on Judgment Day that do not mesh with Jesus' word (Matt. 24:36) that "of that day and hour no one knows."

Certainly John used numbers in ways consistent with the understanding of his people. They were aware of the use of numbers in the Hebrew Scriptures (e.g., Daniel) and in the apocalyptic literature of the times. There were basic meanings for such numbers as 2, 3, 4, 7, 10, and 12 as well as for some of their halves, multiples, squares, cubes and beyond. Thus half of 7 (3 ½) and of 12 (6) will come into play. So will the "multiple" of 6, namely 666. Other examples of multiples frequently used include 70 (7x10); 1,000 (10^3); 12,000 (12x10^3); 1,600 (4^2x10^2); 144 (12^2); 144,000 (12^2x10^3); and 200,000,000 (2x10^4x10^4). The meaning of the key basic numbers and their "spin-offs" is presented below with suggestions for the interpretation of significant passages in Revelation.

BASIC MEANINGS AND SIGNIFICANCE

Two is the number of witness, added strength, or confirmation and validation by repetition. Primary examples are found in Rev. 11:3-12. There the two witnesses are introduced, first through imagery that seems descriptive of Joshua and Zerubbabel (Rev. 11:4). According to Zechariah 2 through 4, where the temple area is also measured with a view toward its preservation, the witnesses are the priestly and royal leaders of the true faith present in Jerusalem. However, Rev. 11:5-6 immediately proceeds to provide added imagery to suggest that Moses and Elijah, often paired in Biblical literature, are also two witnesses,[1] even as the law and the prophets are commonly perceived as God's revelation in the former age. Both examples in Rev. 11 are consistent with the Mosaic concept of "two or three" being the number of witness (Deut. 17:6 and 19:5). The ambiguity of the witnesses' identity leaves the reader with the sense that any grouping of witnesses (Matt. 18:20) who are "faithful unto death" (Rev. 2:10) will receive the Lord's summons (Rev. 11:12) to "come up hither" to receive the crown of life."

Revelation also has an opponent force of two beasts, one from the sea and one from the land (Rev. 13:1-18); they are in cahoots with the dragon (Satan). The beast from the sea is a likely reference to the beastly emperor (Domitian) whose emissaries came by sea to enlist the local authorities (on Asia's land) to enforce the imperial worship. The beast from the land had two horns, suggesting added strength. Without a doubt, it was reinforced in its activity by the beast from the sea, which in turn was empowered by Satan, "the dragon."

Another use of two's, rather unusual, is found in Rev. 20:5-14. The references to the first resurrection and the second death suggest that there are two kinds of each. That would refer to the eternal "death" of the soul that follows the death of the body of the unregenerate; and to the "resurrection" to spiritual life in Christ while on earth, that precedes the bodily resurrection to the fullness of life in heaven for the redeemed.

Thus, death and resurrection are emphasized as central components of the Johannine eschatology. Jesus' death in behalf of mankind was validated by his resurrection. So, also the faithful Christian is enabled to view his own (physical) death as the gateway to a glorious resurrection life when the Lord returns. Revelation 20:4-6 portrays the Christian's entry into God's family as the first resurrection. Those who share in that first (or spiritual) resurrection will not suffer the "second" death (damnation in hell). At the eventual resurrection of the body (the unnamed "second resurrection"), a glorified body joins the soul in order to be forever in the fullness of bliss (1 Cor. 15:42-53). On the other hand, those who will experience the "second death" did not participate in the "first resurrection."

Three is the heavenly number of Hebrew thought. Just as in Christian theology God is thought of as a trinity---Father, Son, and Holy Spirit, so Revelation has several inclusions where the three trinitarian members are alluded to as effective agents of salvation (e.g., Rev. 1:4-6; 1:8-10; 4:2 to 5:6; 14:12-13; and 22:16-19).

A parody on the holy trinity is introduced prominently in Rev. 12-13 where the dragon, thrice foiled, enlists the services of the beasts from the sea and from the land to form an "unholy trinity," as agents of deceit and destruction. The ignominious fate of these three, later referred to as the beast, the false prophet, and the devil (in Rev. 19:19 to 20:10), is that of utter defeat and of being "thrown alive into the lake of fire that burns with brimstone" (Rev. 19:20). There they will "be tormented day and night forever and ever" (Rev. 20:10).

The triumph over Satan within salvation history by 1)Jesus, 2)the angels in heaven, and 3)God's people on earth is told in the three stages of Rev. 12. Likewise, the final or eschatological triumph at the parousia (second coming) is depicted thrice in greater detail as well as in other allusions. Thus, we see it as:

- At Armageddon where the unholy three is seen to employ three foul spirits to summon "the kings of the whole world to assemble for the battle on the great day of God" (Rev. 16:12-21);
- With the heavenly horseman riding forth as King of kings with the armies of heaven to conquer the earthly armies of the beast and the false prophet (those who had sought to deceive and divert "the faithful," Rev. 19:11-21); and

- At "the beloved city" where the fire from heaven quickly consumes the enemy before a battle can even be joined (Rev. 20:7-10).

Three woes are announced "to those who dwell on the earth" (Rev. 8:13). While two of them are described as past (Rev. 9:12; 11:14), the third is prophesied as "soon to come" (Rev. 11:14). That woe is suggested in Rev. 12:12 where the devil has been cast down to earth and sea, coming "in great wrath because he knows that his time is short." The observant reader can assume that that woe too will pass when the devil finally is thrown into the lake of fire and brimstone for his eternal destiny (Rev. 20:10), and when the new heaven and new earth become reality for all the saints (Rev. 21-22).

Counterbalancing the three woes, through which the faithful saints persevere, is the joyous anticipation of the three gates in each of the four walled sides of the holy city, New Jerusalem, heaven. These gates afford entry to the eternal enjoyments inside, described so poetically and magnificently in Rev. 21 and 22.

Truly, three is the divine number, the number of Father, Lamb, and Spirit. Nothing that the three deceivers, Satan, beast, and false prophet can inflict through the three woes and with their assorted sordid wiles "will be able to separate us from the love of God in Christ Jesus our Lord" (Rom. 8:39). After all, heaven's "gates shall never be shut" (Rev. 21:25) to "those who are written in the Lamb's book of life" (Rev. 21:27).

Four is the cosmic, earthly number in Hebrew thought. Thus, the four living creatures that are referenced repeatedly in Revelation (4:6ff.; 6:1ff.; 14:3; and 19:4) represent the animate creaturely order. They are depicted as an inner circle of angels who worship and serve the sovereign Lord who is seated on his throne in glory.

These four living creatures are referred to as the agents for dispatching the four horsemen of the apocalypse who ride forth upon the earth at the opening of the first four (of the seven) seals. These horsemen reveal the hardship and suffering that is the common experience of mankind.

However, there is also much good news in the number four. Despite the arrival of the great day of wrath (Rev. 6:17), there are also four guardian angels. They are pictured as standing at the earth's four corners to hold back the four winds (east, west, north, and south) and to "seal the saints" from destruction in their earthly sojourn (Rev. 7:1-8). These same numberless saints, once sealed, are later described as saved, standing before the throne of God and the Lamb in glory and total bliss (Rev. 7:9-17).

The cosmic sweep of God's sovereignty is again announced at the sixth trumpet blast (Rev. 9:13-21). There the four angels, who are held in readiness at the Euphrates River (Babylon's secure boundary), permit the fury of God's wrath to inflict severe damage and carnage upon "those of mankind who have not the seal of God upon their foreheads" (Rev. 9:4). Here the "sealed" are spared.

Also fortunately, for those who are both "sealed" and "saved," the number four has a promissory, happy aspect. For the New Jerusalem is enclosed by a four-sided wall, with three gates in each side (Rev. 21:12-13). The twelve gates afford entry and all the privileges of membership in the gated-community of the blessed. These have traversed the terrestrial trails and trials and have progressed as pilgrims to arrive at their celestial goal.

Seven is the number indicating perfection. This number represents the joining of the earthly (4) with the heavenly number (3). Revelation includes seven major series of sevens. Four of these are numbered (the 7 letters, seals, trumpets, and bowls); three series of the seven are not (the 7 signs, sights, and beatitudes). In addition, seven is used in many briefer settings in the book.

John delays mentioning the book's villain, Babylon, until chapter 14. Then, he continues to veil the identity of this evil place until three chapters later, where he finally identifies the harlot Babylon through her location on the "seven hills," commonly understood to refer to Rome (Rev. 17:9). A fuller treatment of John's use of seven is given in a later chapter where the three unnumbered series are discussed. Suffice it to say, seven is John's favorite number, used 54 times in Revelation.

Ten is the number of completeness. Thus, there are ten commandments to sum up the law of God. Similarly, ten toes and ten fingers complete the feet and hands, the necessary implements of motion and activity for man. The dragon (12:3), the beast from the sea (13:1), and the scarlet beast (17:3) are all described as having ten horns. This indicates the greatness and sufficiency of their power to work their agendas (as the horn is the symbol for power and strength). The ten diadems (crowns) on the horns of the beast from the sea (Rev. 13:1) refer to its kingly rule. That beast works in concert with the scarlet beast (17:3) which, in turn, is identified with Babylon's ten, or full complement of kings (Rev. 17:12). The kings (in reality emperors) as a group share in the guilt of brutalizing the faithful Christian witnesses of John's churches.[2]

The number ten is also found in multiples such as 1,000; 1,600; 12,000; 144,000; and 200,000,000 which will be exposited briefly below. Whenever the numbers 7 and 10 are used in a series (e.g., Rev. 12:3, 13:1, and 17:3) the distinction between "perfection" and "completeness" blurs a bit, perhaps as another reminder that the numbers are after all only symbols with some fluidity, not to be taken literally in a numeric sense. Elsewhere in Scripture, ten is occasionally multiplied by seven. The resultant 70 indicates totality or infinity as in the comprehensive table of the 70 nations in Genesis 10; or as in Jesus' reply to Peter to forgive the brother "70 times 7" (Matt. 18:22).

Twelve is the number of the faithful, God's chosen people. It was through the children of Israel, the twelve tribes, that salvation history unfolded in the Old Testament. Later, Jesus chose twelve apostles from among his many disciples to anchor his church, which would be "built on the foundation of the apostles and prophets, Christ Jesus himself being the cornerstone" (Eph. 2:20). That same church is declared by Peter to be "a chosen race, a royal priesthood, a holy nation, God's own people" (1 Pet. 2:9).

Revelation 7 employs the imagery of the twelve tribes. There it defines the scope of those who are sealed (verses 1-8), later saved (verses 9-17), as God's own. Interestingly, in listing the twelve tribes, John deliberately substitutes two names from within the "family" for those of Dan and Ephraim. This is for good reason. It was in their two tribal territories that the shrines of Dan and Bethel were located, whose idolatries the prophets regularly condemned. To complete the number of the twelve, John employs instead the name of Levi, whose tribe had received no territorial possession, and the name of Joseph; the latter is a change from the more common pairing of Ephraim with his brother Manasseh. This underscores Revelation's stand against the imperial idolatry which led to the persecution of the saints of Asia.

The number twelve also identifies the woman of Rev. 12:1 as God's people. Fittingly, John's vision reveals her as wearing "on her head a crown of twelve stars." She succeeded in bearing the child, who foiled the murderous dragon by escaping Satan (Herod's plot against the infant Jesus!) and later completed his earthly mission with his triumphant ascension (Rev. 12:4-5).

Likewise, the number twelve is prominent in the vision of the new heaven and the new earth, the site of eternal blessedness of the saints in glory (Rev. 21-22). References to the 12 tribes and 12 apostles (Rev. 21:12-14) support the concept that heaven is for the people of God of all time (both before and after Christ). Appropriately, the holy city's foundations and gates are listed as 12. So also are its measurements, given in multiples of 12, and its embellishments of jewels and pearls (21:12-21). It seems only fitting then that God's faithful in the "paradise restored" finally will be able to enjoy the tree of life's 12 kinds of fruit, yielded in every month of the celestial "year" (Rev. 22:2).

SPIN-OFFS AND MULTIPLES

Three and a half breaks seven in half and negates the concept of perfection. It stands for imperfection, incompleteness, and brokenness. Throughout Revelation it represents the time of suffering, hardship or persecution. That is the reality of life which God's people need to endure as they live out their faith. It reflects what Paul and Barnabas observed when they said "that through many tribulations we must enter the kingdom of God" (Acts 14:23).

This numeric symbol and its variants are concentrated in the middle section of Revelation where the conflict between the witness and his opponents, the "unholy three," is at its most intense level. The Lord's witnesses are described as slain and desecrated for 3½ days, but as also raised and ascending to heaven at the end of these days (Rev. 11:7-12).

More typically, the 3½ is used in reference to years. As in the book of Daniel, the author of Revelation varies the use of this symbol. The informed reader would understand; but the opponents would not. Similarly, Jesus taught in parables so that the disciples would learn without hindrance from the opponents. Accordingly, in Rev. 11:2-3 John refers to 42 months (3½ times 12 months) as the time of trampling of the holy city, and to 1260 days (42 months times 30 days each) as the same period of time for the prophecy of the witnesses. God's faithful people (the woman) will be sustained for these 1260 days of pilgrimage in the wilderness of her earthly life (Rev. 12:6). The same assurance of sustenance for God's persevering saints is repeated in Rev. 12:14 as being for "a time, times (meaning 2), and a half."

The 42 months of blasphemy against God and of warring against the saints (Rev. 13:5) has particular relevance to "the endurance and faith of the saints" (Rev. 13:10) both at John's time and to every age where faith is under trial. In summary, then, for the apocalyptic writer 3½ and its variants depict a troubled time; even so, God is faithful and stands in support of those who persevere. His promise to the church of Smyrna applies to all the saints: "Be faithful unto death, and I will give you the crown of life" (Rev. 2:10).

Six is an evil number. As for many Americans thirteen is perceived to be an "unlucky number," so six was to the Hebrews. It fell short of the perfection of seven like an archer's arrow falls short when it fails to reach its target. It misses the mark. It is the number of sin and of doom. The Greek numeral is fittingly pronounced "hex!" The lament over the utter demise of Babylon is accented by the six-fold repetition of "no more" (ου μη, in Greek, Rev. 18:21-24) and the six-fold use of "alas!" (ου αι, in Greek, also translated "how horrible!" in Rev. 18:10-19). These woeful exclamations denote the tragedy of the obliteration of Babylon, the great city.

By all odds, the most memorable use of six in Revelation is its tripled use in Rev. 13:18, where the number of the beast is given as 666. In effect, it designates the beast (Babylon) as the ultimate evil. Harlot Babylon had dared to try to squelch the worship and service of the Almighty God and to embitter the life of His saints. Can there be any greater presumption or any more heinous evil? In case there is any doubt about the identity of this beast, the reader is clued by the only other appearance of the clause, "this calls for wisdom" (in Rev. 13:18), found in Rev. 17:9. There the wisdom imparted is that the beast is situated on the seven hills (read: Rome)! Of the seven kings that rule there, the one who was currently ruling and was "drunk with the blood of the saints" (Rev. 17:6) is described as the one *between* the fifth and seventh, that is, the *sixth*. Evil indeed! Interpreters perceive this as a reference to Domitian, the one responsible for the empire-wide persecution that afflicted the saints of the churches of Asia to whom John wrote.

Twenty four is one of the four significant "multiples" that builds on the number twelve (144, 144,000, and 12,000 are the others). Rev. 4:4, 10 (and elsewhere in Rev.) refer to 24 thrones on which were seated 24 elders. They represent the redeemed of the Lord of both the former times (Old Testament age) and the latter times (New Testament era). This is after the analogy of the 12 tribes and the 12 apostles, who together add up to 24 and are foundational for and representative of their respective periods.

The 24 elders are consistently depicted in the presence of God, who is enthroned in heaven. There they worship and praise God and the Lamb for the mighty acts of creation and redemption. Their consistent adoration of God gives hope and courage to the saints who are still in the midst of the struggles and trials of their earthly pilgrimage. For the 24 represent those who had "overcome" during their lifetimes, despite hardships and persecution, and were now enthroned in glory. In heaven they could sing their "hallelujahs" and proclaim that God's "judgments are true and just." Their witness encourages the Christian to persevere in times that are wearisome and depressing. Interestingly, Revelation refers ten more times to these elders after chapter 4, for a total of twelve times!

144 and 12,000. **144** is the square of 12, the number of the faithful. The squaring of 12 simply adds emphasis. The wall of New Jerusalem is measured at 144 cubits. Certainly, a wall of 144 cubits far exceeds the height of any protective city wall known to man. It is so designated for the benefit of the faithful. God's people can be assured of perpetual security in the mansion He has prepared (John 14:2) for them in the heavenly city.

Also, the length, breadth, and height of the city are all equal at **12,000** stadia, forming a perfect cube (Rev. 21:16-17). Of course, with 1,000 itself also being the cube of 10 (the complete number), New Jerusalem is viewed as ample in size to accommodate all the saints of all time. With 12 as the number of God's faithful, "12,000" carries the message of God's abundant provision for their future "housing" in heaven! God's presence in the midst of his people was seen in Old Testament times to be in a room that was cube shaped. This was the case for both the tabernacle and the temples, whose "holy of holies" were so described. How appropriate, then, that the highest heaven, God's place, is so depicted. What joy for the persevering saints to know that they may access this previously reserved space and be in the very presence of the King of kings and Lord of lords at his invitation!

144,000 is another spin-off on number 12. It is 12 squared times 10 cubed. The squares and cubes, once again, simply provide greater emphasis to the symbolic meanings of 10 and 12, as noted above. Like the figure twelve thousand, 144,000 stresses the total inclusiveness of all of God's faithful people. Clearly, the literal boundaries of this number cannot contain and delimit the magnitude of its meaning. This number is both superlative and symbolic. It includes all (10^3) of the faithful (12^2) of all times.

There are two passages that refer to God's people which use the symbolic 144,000 (Rev. 7 and 14). In Rev. 7:4-8, in the interlude between the sixth and seventh seal, the faithful people are sealed. They are preserved despite the ravages of time and place. Using the symbol of the 12 tribes, John refers to the divine providence that shields the faithful even in the midst of adversity. This is reminiscent of Jesus' encouragement of his disciples, "Do not fear those who kill the body but cannot kill the soul" (Matt. 10:28). As noted above, the listing of the twelve tribal heads does not include the names of Dan and Ephraim, truly a unique listing! The shrines of Dan and Bethel were in their territories. The theological message is clear. Idolatry is not included under God's protective umbrella. There is only one God who is to be worshipped and honored! All others fall under God's wrath (Rev. 6:12-17).

The numberless throng of Rev. 7:9-17 refers to the saints in glory. In this later vision, John saw the "saved" before the throne of God and the Lamb. Those who are "saved" refer to the same faithful people who earlier had been "sealed" (Rev. 7:3-8). It is as Jesus said in his eschatological discourse, "He who endures to the end will be saved" (Matt. 24:13)[3]

Rev. 14:1-5 includes the other reference to the 144,000. John's vision is that of those redeemed from the earth who are in the presence of God and who sing the "new song" of redemption before the throne with the four living creatures and the elders. This passage closely parallels that of the numberless throng in Rev. 7:9-17.[4] Like Rev. 7, Rev. 14 reassures the faithful, as did Rev. 2:10, that those who are faithful will receive "the crown of life."

OTHER MULTIPLES OF 10

1,000. Of the remaining multiples of ten, the number 1,000 is the one that has drawn the most attention and resulted in the most controversy in the interpretation of Revelation. The expression "a thousand years" is referred to in Revelation only in chapter 20:2-7, where it occurs six times. There is only one other reference to it in the whole New Testament (2 Peter 3:8). As observed previously, 10 is the number indicating completeness. Here it is cubed, simply making more emphatic the fullness of the time required in God's timetable, however long that may be.

Since numbers in apocalyptic literature generally have symbolic value, there is no cogent reason to take the expression "a thousand years" literally as pre-millennialists and post-millennialists do. In fact, to do so leads to various kinds of untenable constructs that have never proved to be reliable.[5] Besides, it leads to trying to "calendar" the date of the second coming---an effort that Jesus declared to be futile (Matt. 24:36). Furthermore, Rev. 20:2-7 defines the "thousand years" as the time frame between the binding and loosing of Satan. That time is well beyond a literal thousand years, as the ensuing discussion will urge.

So, the larger question regarding the length of the "thousand years" is, "How shall we define the time between the binding and loosing of Satan?" Rev. 20:7-10 takes care of denoting the end of the thousand years as the time that Satan is loosed to instigate the end of the earth as we know it. At that time Satan will quickly and decisively be "thrown into the lake of fire and brimstone," hell! According to the teaching of Jesus in the apocalyptic discourses of the Gospels, the end will come suddenly, "as the lightning" (Matt. 24:27) "at an hour you do not expect" (Matt. 24:44).

So then, there remains the question, "When would Satan be bound?" Revelation hints at the binding of Satan as he takes three unsuccessful "swings" in his aggressive attempts to destroy: 1)Jesus; 2)Michael and his angels; and 3)the faithful people of God (chapter 12). For his efforts, Satan is "out" after three "strikes" and stands "on the sand of the sea" (Rev. 12:17) in the hopes that the intermediaries, on whom he now depends, can be more successful.

A clearer portrait of Satan's binding can be found in John 12:23-33. There Jesus reflects on his crucifixion as the time of glorification of himself and of the Father. The Father's response from heaven signals yet further glorification. In that context Jesus refers to the *casting out* of "the ruler of this world" and of his own "lifting up" by which he would draw all men to himself. Rev. 20:2 draws on the same Greek verb ($\beta\alpha\lambda\lambda\omega$) to refer to Satan's being *thrown* into the pit.[6]

Regarding this period of indeterminate length, Brighton succinctly summarizes the consistent witness of the Gospels, stating that

"the millennium began with the binding of Satan at Christ's first advent (his incarnation, ministry, death, resurrection, and ascension) and will conclude when Christ returns in glory to bring this present world to its end."[7]

The numbers **200,000,000** and **1,600,** while meaningful, have netted less ink from commentators. Yet each gives forth its own message. At the blast of the sixth trumpet, a cavalry of "twice ten thousand times ten thousand" (**200,000,000**) is released at the dreaded boundary of the Euphrates River, which Rome's armies never had been able to cross.[8] The massive slaughter of "a third of mankind" (Rev. 9:13-18) that followed was directed at the unrepentant oppressors of God's people. Even that debacle failed to move to repentance the hearts of the idolatrous survivors (Rev. 9:20-21). This numberless throng (a virtual doubling of infinity) focuses on the inevitability of the ultimate destruction of the murderous and unrepentant opponents of the people of God. It foreshadows the more transparent message of Rev. 18, which portrays "Babylon's" fall and the resulting mournful lament over that city's demise. John's message is clear. In the end, God will use the means at hand to bring to judgment those who persecute His people!

1,600. The judgment scene of Rev. 14:17-20 culminates in the treading of the winepress of the wrath of God outside the city. It seizes on the prophetic pictures from Joel 3:13 and Isaiah 63:1-6. These present the Vindicator of God's people as having trodden the winepress alone in his wrath, with resultant staining of his garments from the lifeblood of the opponents. In John's vision, this picture is repeated, and it adds the detail that the blood of the grapes flowed forth "as high as horse's bridle, for the 1,600 stadia" (Rev. 14:20). The number 1,600 is the product of 4^2 times 10^2. The meaning relates to the fullness (10 times 10, completeness compounded!) of God's wrath against the sinful unrepentant earthlings (4 times 4, emphatic use of the cosmic or earthly number). In plain English, it refers to God's utter judgment upon the evil on earth (much in the same way as Rev. 19-20 refers to the total slaughter of the opposition armies which are in league with the dragon, Satan).[9]

The detail about the "horse's bridle" in Rev. 14:20 takes on added significance in Rev. 19:11-16 where the rider on the white horse, namely Jesus, is "clad in a robe dipped in blood." Obviously, this King of kings is the one who had trodden the winepress of God's wrath alone on Calvary's cross as there he bled to redeem mankind from the penalty of their sins.

Concluding thought.   Suffice it to say, the numbers of the Apocalypse, while confusing to those who might oppress the readers of John's letters to the churches, were meaningful to his intended audience. Thankfully, their use served John's original readers well. They can be useful vehicles of meaning for modern day readers as well as they promote the "good news!" Praise God!

---

[1]Elijah is associated with the drought at King Ahab's time, recorded in 1 Kings 17-18, which James 5:17 says lasted "for three and a half years." Moses served as agent of the ten plagues of Egypt, described in Exodus 7-11.

[2]Emperor worship was widespread in the first century.   For information regarding the various temples in the cities of Asia, dedicated to the worship of Roman emperors, see Krodel, Revelation, pages 104-148; and Blake and Edmonds, Biblical Sites in Turkey, pages 117-141.

[3]The suggestion of some religionists that exactly and literally 144,000 will be in heaven, and that those who are saved after that quota was reached will spend eternity in a renovated earthly sphere separate from those in heaven has no basis in Scripture.

[4]If only a literal 144,000 will be in heaven, as Jehovah's Witnesses profess, then one would have to take the earthly Mount Zion (Rev. 14:1) literally as being in heaven also.   However, the innumerable multitude of Rev. 7:9 is before the same throne as the 144,000 of Rev. 14! Clearly, it seems to be John's intent to show the number of the "saved" to be the same as those "sealed," an infinite number that includes all the faithful.

[5]Instructive in this regard is the book by Plueger, Things to Come for Planet Earth.   Also helpful is "A Lutheran Response to the Left Behind Series," CTCR Report of the LCMS.

[6]Brighton, <u>Revelation</u>, pages 548-549, comes to the same conclusion by referring to Matt. 12:22-29 and parallels. He notes that Jesus cast out demons, showing his dominance over and his *binding* of the strong man (Satan).

[7]<u>Ibid</u>., page 533.

[8]Lindsey and Carlson in <u>The Late Great Planet Earth</u> (pages 81-87) argue that the 200,000,000 is a literal number which the Chinese militia can and will fulfill. However, even if the number were to be taken literally, it fails to deal with the question of where China would get 200,000,000 horses. The vision is about cavalry, not infantry!

[9]Translations such as the NASB, the NAB, and the NRSV miss the scope and significance of this point by paraphrasing the symbolic number 1,600 as "200 miles."

CHAPTER IV

THE SEVEN LETTERS

John's letters to the seven churches of Asia are found in Revelation 2 and 3. The selection of exactly seven churches, their geographic arc along main roads, and their stylized form all suggest that these are messages intended for all the churches of Asia. The other churches of Asia would be instructed and inspired by the messages applied to their seven kindred churches. Similarly, the church universal of all ages would benefit. That the whole Christian church is the target audience of the letters is also suggested by the repetition in each letter of "He who has an ear, let him hear what the Spirit says to the churches (plural). These messages are an integral part of the whole book and reflect both backward to the imagery of the Christological vision of chapter one, as well as forward to the fulfillment near the end of Revelation. The repetition and the symmetry of the seven letters lends a poetic quality to these letters in a way somewhat reminiscent of the creation story in Genesis with its 7-day framework.

The letters impress on the church the need for persistent endurance in a time of persecution. Christians are encouraged to persevere patiently in the face of threats both internal and external. While the internal threats include various kinds of temptations that cause backsliding, the external ones are more obvious and immediate. Thus, the main tension of the book is in the conflict of interest between worship of Christ only or of Caesar in addition. Despite impending persecution, Christians are urged to hold fast the confession of faith and to be ready to sacrifice for it if required.

Recent commentators are largely agreed that the pattern of the letters exhibits considerable uniformity, including a geographic address, a Christological identification, points of praise and of reproach, followed by some promise and a stylized concluding exhortation. However, they are not uniformly agreed on the number of constituent parts each letter has. Thus, Heidt gives five parts; Dawn and Onstad six; Becker, Metzger, Morris, and Murphy, seven.

My own study has led me to identify <u>eight</u> characteristic parts <u>within</u> the seven letters, and to list <u>two additional unstated ones</u> which were obvious in the life and times of these seven historic churches. My two addenda pertain to the cultural background of the churches named and the contemporary application to faith and life for the church universal. The latter two parts are reflected in #2 and #10 of my accompanying chart of the seven churches. Additionally, I believe that I am breaking <u>new ground</u> by positing the inclusion of <u>both</u> a word of <u>challenge and</u> one of <u>confrontation</u>. The challenge is a simple declaration of what the churches are expected to do. The confrontational word advises them of the consequences if they don't do it. In the case of Smyrna and Philadelphia, the two churches which are not served with a word of condemnation or reproof, the word of confrontation is directed toward the opponent "synagogue of Satan." Finally, I have listed <u>a post-script</u>, found in the closing chapters of Revelation. It indicates or <u>reiterates future fulfillment</u> of the promise(s), or words of consolation, given within the body of the letters.

Since the literature on the letters is so voluminous already, and in many ways very complete, my approach is simple and direct. It offers an expanded chart with several added considerations, not included in others' formatted charts.

<u>The approach</u> will be to give special attention first to the cultural background of the letters, and then to show the relationship of that background and the Christology to other parts of the letters. (Of particular interest in each of the letters is the close correlation of the word of "consolation" or promise with the "completion of the promise" statement; see Boxes 8 and P.S. on the accompanying chart.) Then, some contemporary applications reflect on the letters' message in terms of their goals, the perceived threats to the goals, and the gospel rescue points.

Each letter begins with the commission: "to the angel of the church in . . . write." The word "angel" is used in a sense here that differs from its use elsewhere in the Apocalypse where angels are God's *celestial* messengers or agents. Here "angel" seems to refer to a *human* messenger directly involved in the spiritual care of the particular church. However one may try to define the term more

THE LETTERS TO THE SEVEN CHURCHES

CONTENT	Chapter 2:1-7	Chapter 2:8-11	Chapter 2:12-17
1. Commission (to write to:)	EPHESUS	SMYRNA	PERGAMUM
2. Cultural Background	Paul's mission center for Asia; John, bishop later. Temples of Diana & emperor; theater; harbor, hub for 3 roads	Izmir: beauteous city! acropolis (crown); *Dea Roma* temple; harbor, trade center; Polycarp, bishop, martyr; games	Seleucid capital; 1000' cone hill; Asklepios, Zeus, Dionysius, & caesar temples; library, parchment; *ius gladii*
3. Christology	Holds the 7 stars; and, walks among the 7 lampstands	The first & the last; the one Who died & came to life	The one with the sharp, two-edged sword
4. Commendation	Endurance; keeping faith pure; hating Nicolaitans	Enduring tribulation, poverty, & slander of "pseudo-Jews"	Holding to Jesus' name & faith; Antipas, "my faithful witness"
5. Condemnation (Criticism)	Growing lax regarding their first love	NONE	Harboring false teachings (Balaam and the Nicolaitans)
6. Challenge	Remember from what you've fallen! Repent!	Don't fear the coming suffering! Be faithful unto death!	Repent!
7. Confrontation (Consequences)	If not, I will remove your lampstand!	["Synagogue of Satan" is exposed for its slander & cruelty.]	If not, I will war vs. the transgressors with the sword of my mouth!
8. Consolation (Promise)	Eating of the tree of life in the paradise of God	Getting the crown of life; not being hurt by the second death	The hidden manna, the white stone, & a new name
9. Concluding Admonition	Let him who has an ear hear what the Spirit says!	Let him who has an ear hear what the Spirit says!	Let him who has an ear hear what the Spirit says!
10. Contemporary Application	When our priorities are blurred, we need to re-focus on our first love to nurture & extend it.	Despite adversity, we need to be faithful to God, Whose promises are for eternal life. (*"per aspera ad astra"*)	In the face of perverse teachings and external pressures, we need to be uncompromising on God's revealed truth.
P. S. Completion (of the promise)	The tree of life...for the healing of the nations (22:2)	Over such the second death has no power.... book of life (20:6,12)	His name shall be on their foreheads (22:4)

THE LETTERS TO THE SEVEN CHURCHES (CONTINUED)

Chapter 2:18-29	Chapter 3:1-6	Chapter 3:7-13	Chapter 3:14-22
THYATIRA	SARDIS	PHILADELPHIA	LAODICEA
Seleucid frontier city, guarding the empire; many trade guilds with religious rites; home of Lydia (Acts 16)	Lydian capital; "safe" on 1500' citadel? it fell twice! wool; temples of Artemis & Cybele (restorer of the dead?)	"Open door" to Greek culture, "gateway to East"; commercial center; many earth-quakes; renamed twice	Money, manufacture, & medicine; warm mineral springs; key road juncture; emperor worship; Col. 4:16
Son of God; eyes like a flame of fire; feet like burnished bronze	Having the 7 spirits of God & the 7 stars	The holy & true one who has the key of David	The "Amen," faithful & true witness, beginning of God's creation
Increase of works: love, faith, service, & patient endurance	NONE	Having kept Jesus' word, and not denied His name	NONE
Tolerating Jezebel's false teachings (immorality & idolatry)	Being called alive, while really dead	NONE	Being lukewarm, smug in riches & prosperity
Hold fast what you have; avoid the "deep things" of Satan!	Repent! Revitalize your works! Awake!	Hold fast what you have so no one seizes your crown!	Buy from the "Amen" gold, garments & salve! Repent; and open the door!
"Impenitents" will suffer sickness, tribulation, & their children's death.	If not, I will come like a thief, at an unknown hour.	["Synagogue of Satan" will acknowledge you & see my love for you.]	I'll spit you out. You are wretched, poor, pitiable, blind, & naked.
Getting power over the nations, rule with rod of iron, & the Morning Star	Be clad in white; name in book of life; stand before God & angels	Safe in hour of trial; pillar in God's temple; get thrice-holy name	Eating with Jesus and sitting with Him on His throne
Let him who has an ear hear what the Spirit says!	Let him who has an ear hear what the Spirit says!	Let him who has an ear hear what the Spirit says!	Let him who has an ear hear what the Spirit says!
When the church is corrupted from within, we need to dig deeper into God's word.	When faith becomes smug & inactive, we need an infusion of God's Spirit.	When doors seem to close and hopes wane, we need to trust God's power & promise to keep doors open.	When self-sufficiency dulls our eagerness for grace, we need to see reality & invite Jesus in to give us true riches.
They shall reign for-ever...I, Jesus...bright morning star (22:5,16)	Name... written in the Lamb's book of life (20:15; 21:27)	temple is God & Lamb; name on foreheads (21:3,22; 22:4)	I saw thrones; tree of life...yielding its fruit (20:4; 22:2)

narrowly, one thing is clear: the message given the church's "angel" is intended to be communicated and applied to the faith and life of that church, whether that be Ephesus or any of the other churches.

EPHESUS

(REV. 2:1-7)

1. CULTURAL BACKGROUND.

In John's time, Ephesus was the chief city of the province of Asia. It was the hub for three major roads that stretched inland from there to the other cities. As the main Asian harbor for Roman ships, Ephesus came to be known as the "Highway to Rome," connecting land and sea routes. The goddess Roma and several emperors, including Domitian, were honored there. Its most renowned temple, that of Diana (the fertility goddess, known to the Greeks as Artemis), was one of the "Seven Wonders of the World." This temple was a center of crime and immorality, as criminals sought asylum here, and hundreds of sacred prostitutes were attached to the temple. Not surprisingly, then, the letter denounces the Nicolaitans, who taught that Christians could eat food dedicated to the honor of idols and could engage in sexual immorality in the name of religion. The theater, which seated 25,000 in a city of 250,000, was the site of the riot of the silversmiths related in Acts 19, where Paul barely escaped with his life.

St. Paul had planted the mission in Ephesus and in the rest of Asia, and was succeeded there by Timothy. Later, John became bishop of the church in Ephesus and served it for several decades up to his exile on Patmos. Irenaeus affirms that Polycarp, later bishop of Smyrna, had been a personal disciple of John.

2. INTERRELATIONSHIPS ARE SEEN BY A VERTICAL VIEW OF VARIOUS PARTS OF THE CHART.

The Christological "word" (hereafter referred to as #3, as seen on the chart) relates to the word of confrontation (box #7). Jesus is the one who owns and guards the church's "angel" (or spiritual messenger) with the authority and power of "his right hand." He walks in the presence of the churches which serve as lampstands, or bearers, of the

Light. The reader will understand that Christ is the Light of the World (see John 8:12; 9:5), and thus, the church is where His presence and His word are found, applied, and shared. The confrontational element of the letter (box #7) suggests that the refusal to repent (i.e., to rekindle their first love) will lead to the church's dissolution (or, in John's words: their lampstand will be removed). For, when the gospel "Light" is no longer beaming forth there to legitimize the proper function of the "lampstands" as Light bearers, they are rendered obsolete and are removed. Without love, there is no church. As the popular song has it, "they will know we are Christians by our love!"

Secondly, the word of consolation (or promise, #8) draws on the concept of eating from the tree of life in God's paradise. This tree had been put off limits to fallen man (Gen. 3:22-24). The good news of the book is that in John's vision of the New Jerusalem, where God's blessed ones will be with Him forever after the judgment, the tree of life is accessible. Additionally, its fruit of "twelve kinds" is abundant, "yielding its fruit each month," with *healing* in its leaves (Rev. 22:2; see the P.S. box). This is a significant advance over the fig leaf aprons (of Genesis 3) which covered the *shame* of fallen mankind. In heaven, nothing good will be denied those who will walk in the presence of Him Who had "walked" among their lampstands during their earthly sojourn (box #3).

3. CONTEMPORARY APPLICATIONS.

Goal: Remember that first love! Recall that fervor we had when we first realized that we were God's own, that He held us firmly in His loving hands! That fervor regarding God's love needs continual re-focus, nurture, and sharing. (It is too good to hoard and to keep from others.) Also, remain strong in the face of false teachers and corrupting influences (e.g., the Nicolaitans, who perverted the worship life through idolatrous and adulterous practices).

Threat: When we lose our first love, we forget the motivation for loving others. When the incomparable love "that passes human understanding" which Jesus showed by His life and ministry loses its glow, it is easy to grow lax in reciprocating devotion to God and His people and to become preoccupied with self.

Rescue: Christ holds us personally in His caring hands, even while He sits at the Father's right hand. He keeps His promise of being with us "even to the close of the age" through the Holy Spirit Whom He has given us, and Who inhabits our bodies as His temple. Thus, He walks among us as the Light of the World, enabling us to be lampstands, holders and bearers of that precious gospel light (the Light of the World) which illuminates those who enter our presence and participate in our walk of faith.

4. CONCLUDING THOUGHT.

We need to keep a clear focus on God's great love for us. We need to resist false theologies and cultural influences that would distract or divert our walk with Jesus. To do that, we need a continual renewal in God's word and sacraments. Then we will have the power to extend our walk with the Lord and include others in it.

SMYRNA

(REV. 2:8-11)

1. CULTURAL BACKGROUND.

Smyrna was reputed as among the most beautiful cities of antiquity. It rose from obscurity when Lysimachus rebuilt it in 190 B.C. It was a rare planned city of its time, built according to plans attributed to Alexander the Great. It had an excellent harbor to the sea on the west and had roads to the east, situating it well as a trade center. A temple for the goddess Roma was built there in 195 B.C., probably the first such temple. Its constant *faithful*ness to Rome was rewarded by rare privileged permission to build a temple to Emperor Tiberius in 26 A.D.[1] So, it had two temples honoring the imperial cult before the time of the apostle John, more than any other city of its time! The citadel or *crown* of the city, rising majestically to the east, had several temples. Smyrna was regarded by many as the crown of Asia.

St. Paul's influence likely led to the beginnings of the church of Smyrna, as one can conclude from Acts 19:10. There Luke writes regarding Paul's two-year stay in Ephesus that "all the residents of Asia heard the word of the Lord." Here also later Polycarp, bishop of Smyrna, would suffer martyrdom in the second century for his refusal to worship the emperor as "Lord and God."

2. INTERRELATIONSHIPS SEEN FROM THE TEXT (AND THE CHART).

The cultural background (box 2) alludes to the city's "crown" and its long-time fidelity to Rome. John challenges the church (see box 6) to be faithful unto death. The city had come to life spectacularly from a kind of death of over three centuries. Even more significantly, Christ rose from the dead (box 3) with eternal consequences for His people. While Smyrna may be the crown of Asia, Jesus promises the crown of life, safety from harm by the second death (box 8).

Christology. As already noted, the One who died and conquered death (box 3) emboldens the faithful with the twin challenge to fear neither suffering nor death (box 6). Their reward is the promise (box 8) of the crown of life; that is, avoiding the second death (damnation) while gaining eternal life.

Smyrna is one of only two churches (with Philadelphia) to escape criticism (box 5). The obverse is that she is commended (box 4) for her suffering of poverty and the slander by false Jews. It is the church's opponents who are confronted and exposed (box 7) as being in league with Satan. The good news, such as it is, in regard to their tribulation, is that their suffering will be brief, "ten days." Regarding such as the faithful of Smyrna, Rev. 20:6 and 12 reaffirm that "over such the second death has no power" because their names are in "the book of life," and they will have the "crown of life" (see the P.S. box).

3. CONTEMPORARY APPLICATIONS.

Goal: Be faithful, life-long! Don't fear suffering or death for your faith! Be strong amid testing. Take the long view. Fix your eyes on the reward God has promised in the hereafter. Attain to the crown of life.

Threat: Surrendering the faith and forfeiting eternal life by
- Caving in to pressure from faithless peers
- Buckling under to societal slander and testing
- Compromising the faith by following immoral laws and leaders.[2]

Rescue: God knows our suffering and cares deeply. So deeply, in fact, that Jesus died for us so that we can escape the second death and rise to eternal life, even as He rose from death to life. His faithfulness inspires our faithfulness. His suffering of slander and tribulation was rewarded by the crown of life. We have the same promise and prospect for our fidelity.

4. CONCLUDING THOUGHT.

Jesus is "the first and the last, the Alpha and the Omega" (2:8; 1:8). His conquest of death emboldens us to remain faithful and to overcome the thrusts of a hostile earthly environment ("a synagogue of Satan," 2:9). We have excellent models for life in such as the apostle John, bishop Polycarp, and Jesus Himself. Hebrews 13:13-14 encapsulates the message of Smyrna's church: "Therefore, let us go forth to him outside the camp, bearing abuse for him." (John, Polycarp, and Jesus all did!) "For here we have no lasting city, but we seek the city which is to come."

PERGAMUM

(REV. 2:12-17)

1. CULTURAL BACKGROUND.

The Seleucids controlled the region of Asia after the death of Alexander the Great. They made Pergamum their capital and controlled it until 133 B.C. when it was ceded to the Romans at the death of King Attalus III. It remained a principal city of the Roman province of Asia well past the time of John. Its citadel, a conical hill, rose 1,000 feet above the surrounding plain.

Pergamum's claim to international fame was its huge library which housed 200,000 parchment scrolls. In antiquity, only Alexandria had a greater library. The rivalry between these two cities led to the invention of parchment at Pergamum. This was spurred when Pergamum tried to lure away Alexandria's librarian, and Alexandria in turn put an embargo on papyrus exports.

Pergamum was also preeminent in Asia for its famous temples, dedicated variously to Greco-Roman gods, emperors, and Asklepios, the god of healing. The most famous Greek temple in Pergamum was that of Zeus, whose altar was dedicated by King Attalus I after he defeated the Galatians in a battle that solidified the independence of the kingdom of Pergamum. The temple of Zeus was one of the Seven Wonders of the Ancient World. Roman religion was most problematic for the church in John's time because of the renewed emphasis on emperor worship.

Again, Pergamum was on the forefront as the first Asian city permitted to dedicate a temple to an emperor (Augustus, in 29 A.D.). Several other emperors were later honored with temples and an annual worship ritual requirement.

Perhaps the most valued temple of the area was that of Asklepios, the god of healing, whose symbol was the serpent. Since many mental patients from near and far found cures through psychic suggestion of the priests and their snake-induced shock therapy, Asklepios received the title Soter, Savior. The serpent subsequently became a symbol of healing in the medical profession. However, for Christians, it is shocking that anyone other than Jesus should be considered as Savior of the world. In the Bible, the serpent is a Satanic symbol (Gen. 3; Num. 21; John 3; Rev. 12 and 20).

"Satan's throne" (2:13) is thought by some to be the massive and impressive altar of Zeus; by others, the temple of an emperor or of Asklepios (the serpent Savior). Most likely, however, it refers to all of the above or primarily to the imperial temples which were the chief reason for persecution of the Christians of Asia. Refusal to worship the emperor was considered treason in this polytheistic society. At this time Christians were called "atheists" for their refusal to worship the Greco-Roman gods (and emperors). The local authorities in Pergamum had the ius gladii, "the right of the sword," which permitted them to inflict the death penalty; this would clearly cause great distress for faithful Christians who were regarded as disrespectful of local religious decrees (see Daniel for parallels). Already Antipas, a faithful witness, had suffered death for his profession of faith (2:13).

2. INTERRELATIONSHIPS WITHIN PARTS OF THE LETTER.

The Christological description (#3) refers to "him who has the sharp two-edged sword." The point is that the faithful should not fear the local officials who wield the sword by the ius gladii, but rather fear the One whose two-edged sword is the key to life that extends to eternity (see also Gen. 3:24 and Rev. 22:2 regarding the sword and the tree; and Heb. 4:12). Transgressors are warned and confronted (#7) with the sword of Christ's mouth (His word of judgment).

The commendation is for the faithful (#4) who hold to Jesus' name alone, even unto death (as did Antipas, "my witness"). The faithful witness is one who dares to be counter-cultural and politically incorrect even in a city known for being "Satan's throne," the place "where Satan dwells," and the center of worship of Caesar and other deities (#2).

The consolation of the Christians (#8) is that they are promised *hidden manna, a white stone, and a new name.* The promised manna, may refer to the contrast between eating unclean foods (those dedicated to false deities) and receiving God's gracious sustenance, such as the manna from heaven (as in the Exodus wanderings) or the Bread of Life which Jesus offered His followers (John 6). Promise also comes through the picture of the white stone, which at one time was a symbol of exoneration, while a black stone indicated guilt. Thus, the white stone may be an allusion to the vindication of the Christian before the great white throne of God (Rev. 20); there the verdict is rendered to favor those whose names are written in the book of life, in sharp contrast to the negative judgment given by the earlier imperial persecutors. Finally, the "new name" is likely the same as that of the Father and the Lamb, inscribed on the foreheads of the redeemed on Mt. Zion and in the New Jerusalem (14:1 and 22:4; see the P.S. box). The faithful in Pergamum had been commended for holding fast to the name of Jesus. They are distinguished from those who worship the imperial beast and who name him as "Dominus et Deus," Lord and God (13:13-18).

3. CONTEMPORARY APPLICATIONS.

Goal: The Christians are called to be faithful witnesses, of which Antipas was the prototype. The witness (Greek, martys, from which the word "martyr" is derived) is one who confesses Jesus only as Savior (Soter), and who will not condone or tolerate false teachings and pagan practices in the family of faith. (For the glorification of the witness who has walked along the pathway of suffering to his goal, see also Rev. 11:1-13.)

Threat. The problem of Pergamum is opposite that of Ephesus. The latter had stood strong against errorists, but had lost their erstwhile spiritual fervor, their first love. In contrast, the Pergamese Christians had tolerated spiritual aberrations (Balaam and the Nicolaitans), thinking that taking a firm stand might compromise love. Clearly, teachings and life-styles that compromise the confession, worship, and discipleship of Jesus the Savior must be opposed with both love and firmness.

Rescue. Gospel vehicles here include three pictures:
   A. The hidden manna. This is a reminder of God's sustenance during *earthly* life (e.g., manna in the wilderness), and into *eternal* life (Jesus, the Bread of Life). The "hidden manna" (missing after the temple and its ark were destroyed) comes into full view again when the Lord returns (for Jesus is God's incarnate tabernacle and the Living Bread—John 1:14; 2:19-21; and 6:32-35); and, He will return! Along similar lines, the fruit from the tree of life will become available in heaven to the faithful (Rev. 22:2), who will live forever after in the perfect life of the saints in glory.

B. A white stone. There is vindication and final victory before God's great white throne for those who have overcome the Satanic detractors and distractions, and who have followed Jesus faithfully unto death. Theirs is the crown of life. They are God's people in the bliss of the New Jerusalem (Rev. 21:3-7).

C. A new name. The name of God and the Lamb (14:1) is a badge of honor and blessing for those who refused to be associated with the name and the mark of the beast (13:17-18), which designated those who worshiped false deities, including emperors, or pursued alternate paths to salvation. Those receiving the new name will bask in the joys of Mt. Zion and the New Jerusalem. Those who once were called Christian as a term of derision will now feel honored to be so named. Those once called "atheists" by the imperial persecutors will be declared to be "His people" and will experience His presence (21:3).

4. CONCLUDING THOUGHT.

In the face of perverse teachings and external secular threats, we need an uncompromising stand on God's revealed truth as revealed in Jesus. Basic instruction in and study of the truth of the Scriptures enables discernment of errorists and joyful sharing and defense of the faith. The example of time-honored heroes of the faith nurtures spirituality (see Heb. 11-12). So does the example of contemporary spiritual stalwarts, such as Antipas was for Pergamum (Rev. 2:13). Love for others will spur Christians to manifest the One who alone is the Savior, the way, the truth, and the life. He uniquely revealed and exemplified the love of God (1 John 4:14-16).

THYATIRA

(REV. 2:18-29)

1. CULTURAL BACKGROUND.

The message to Thyatira covers 12 verses, is the longest of the seven letters, and is written to the most obscure of the seven cities. Only scant ruins remain to reveal its past history. Even so, it dramatizes the danger facing the Christians of Asia, as graphically revealed in Rev. 13:17-18 where "the beast" limits the uncompromising faithful Christians' ability to "buy and sell."

Strategically, Thyatira served as a buffer city, guarding the path to Pergamum, the capital of the province. Thyatira was on the road which connected Pergamum with cities to the southeast, including Sardis, Philadelphia, Laodicea, and points beyond. Travel and trade from the East came through her to connect with the West. This made her a center of commerce, a place where trade guilds flourished. Lydia, "a seller of purple goods," had come from this city and was Paul's first European convert of note at Philippi (Acts 16:14).

Each guild was associated with a patron deity. To not join a guild would seriously threaten one's prosperity, or even survival, in business. The guilds were bonded together by common meals in which there was a sacrifice to the patron god. Generally, when the feast ended, the "fun" began, spiced with sexual license. To walk away to avoid the latter would expose one to ridicule and discrimination, also in the market place. The threat to the faith was complicated by a self-styled prophetess, referred to as Jezebel, who pleaded for compromise with secular standards in the interest of commercial prosperity. She typified the church's universal question: "Can the Christian compromise with the world in matters of faith and life?"

2. INTERRELATIONSHIPS SEEN FROM THE TEXT (AND CHART):

The cultural background (see box 2) intersects with the condemnation and challenge directed to the church of Thyatira (see boxes 5 and 6). On the one hand, the religious rites of the local trade guilds included participation in words and acts of idolatry and adultery. An impenitent spiritual leader there was following in the footsteps of the ancient Jezebel, King Ahab's queen, who misled her husband and the kingdom of Israel in fostering the worship of the Canaanite fertility god, Baal. She had approved of acts viewed by God's people as cultic sexual immorality on the premise that nature would reciprocate with a kind of corresponding fertility of the soils and crops. After all, the logic went, could not one still hold to the worship of the Lord, even if engaging in an occasional service to the deity that was held to foster economic success and survival? Besides, could the engagement in a rare sex act to the honor of the patron deity be bad if it promoted a perceived greater good? Such "deep things" of God, as championed by the false prophetess of Thyatira, were seen in John's "prophecy," in reality, to be the "deep things" of Satan!

The church in this place is criticized for tolerating their influential "Jezebel." She deserved rebuke! John warned that those who follow her will be punished severely with sickness, great tribulation, and death unless they repent (the challenge of verses 22-23, see box 7). One cannot worship and serve both God and mammon!

Christology. The term, "Son of God," is used only once in Revelation (2:18, see box 3) to refer to Jesus. It powerfully asserts that Jesus sees with power to act where the local deity, Apollo, has limits and flaws. This is depicted through allusion to His eyes and feet.[3]

The "eyes like a flame of fire" (2:18) suggest the ability to penetrate to the core of the motive for tolerating the influence of Jezebel, namely the avoidance of persecution while compromising one's faith. The fiery eyes also suggest the divine anger over the prevailing sin. His gaze penetrates both the "kidneys and hearts," a reference to the seat of emotions (kidneys) and thoughts (heart). Man cannot hide even the innermost feeling and thought from His pervasive gaze.

Jesus' feet are described as of fine bronze. That suggests the power of the Risen Christ, who by His conquest of death has put all things under his feet as He sits victoriously at the right hand of the Father (see boxes 3 and 8). He alone possesses all power and is able to dispense it to those "who keep [His] works until the end" (v. 26, see box 6). He will exercise His rule over all powers, even that of the Roman imperial potentate! He can easily smash the sturdiest pottery of the miscreant tradesmen with His "rod of iron," an analogy readily understood by the guild members in Thyatira. The Christians, of course, know of that power which the Father shared with Jesus (v. 27, see also Ps. 2:8-9).

The ultimate bonus for the faithful is the receipt of the morning star (v. 28, see also the P.S. box, Rev. 22:16, where the allusion is to Jesus). This is a rare use in Revelation of the Lord's personal name, Jesus. What greater gift can there be than to receive Jesus Himself? Some have seen in this metaphor the promise of resurrection. As William Barclay noted, "As the morning star rises over the darkness of the night, so the Christian will rise over the darkness of death."[4]

3. CONTEMPORARY APPLICATIONS.

Goal: To fix one's eyes on the priceless gift of God's grace and power. This implies several things for latter-day "Thyatiran" Christians. It involves:

- recognizing and trusting the unique God of grace and power as the only one who can and does give eternal life (John 3:16; 14:6).
- avoiding corrupting influences and behaviors (e.g., idolatry or syncretistic worship, promiscuous sexuality, and discrimination against or persecution of the innocent and upright).
- confronting the evils of society in the interest of freeing God's people for lives of responsible service.
- continuing, despite existing evils, in the practice of good works and patient endurance.

Threat: The pull of sin with its allurements. Temptations have multiplied as earthlings continue their descending spirals into the brothels of secularity, often unaware that this is sin and that its wage is death. The blessings of multiculturalism and the acceptance of diversity have been dimmed and diverted by the champions of the philosophy that "anything goes" as long as it works for you and/or feels good. Other gods, or life-shaping influences, are widely accepted as equal in value or more desirable than the plan of God for grace and glory. The motive power of economic gain leads to blurring of the parameters of morality, justice, and human compassion.

Rescue: Patient endurance in the ways of God, fueled by faith in His gracious promise, leads to a life of confident and joyous fulfillment. The promises of God include:
- *power* from the omnipotent One for His faithful flock to uplift them in their temporary stressful moments of being ridiculed or oppressed.
- *rule* with the King of kings, who will finally put all enemies under His powerful feet (which are like "burnished bronze"); with a "rod of iron" (unlimited power) He will smash all perverted cultic and cultural forces.
- *light* from the morning star, which is Jesus Christ himself (Rev. 22:16). He will dispel the darkness of sin and death with the power of the resurrection. That will terminate all ambiguity, persecution, and powerlessness. As Barclay put it, "The Christian life, even at its hardest and darkest, looks, not to the sunset, but to the dawn."[5]

4. CONCLUDING THOUGHT.

Those within the Christian community are, nevertheless, also in the world. The call of the faithful is not to avoid the world, but to shun the worldly ways engendered by the evil one (John 17:15). "When temptations come alluring," the church prays, "make us patient and enduring."

Modern Jezebels continue to entice, but can only offer fleeting "benefits," destined for early bankruptcy. In contrast, Christians are challenged to walk in the Light of the world as they look for the daybreak of a glorious eternity. Then they will experience the fullness of being "more than conquerors through Him who loved us" (Rom. 8:37).

SARDIS

(REV. 3:1-6)

1. CULTURAL BACKGROUND.

Sardis is the story of past splendor and present decay. History reveals that before Jerusalem fell to the Babylonians in 586 B.C., Sardis was already a great city of unlimited wealth. The Lydian King Croesus, who ruled from 570-546 B.C. was reputed to be the richest man on earth. He believed that his city, built on a spur of Mt. Tmolus, 1,500 feet above the surrounding plain, was impregnable. Yet, in a war with King Cyrus of Persia, the city fell because a Persian soldier, Hyeroeades, observed a Sardian soldier coming down the steep hill to retrieve a helmet, and then going up the cliff-like rise again by way of a crevice. That night the Persian was able to scale the hill by the same route with a band of soldiers. The sleeping city fell because it had no watchmen on duty. The Sardians had felt so safe that they posted no guards. That is why the words "awake" and "watch" are so fitting in the letter to the church in Sardis. Several centuries later Sardis came under Greek rule and culture. Then, after Alexander's death, the Seleucid king, Antiochus III, lay siege to it. The unguarded city fell again to a surprise nocturnal attack.

The Sardians built a second city on the roomier plain below the nearly impenetrable city on the citadel. It had a temple dedicated to the goddess Artemis, built soon after the time of King Croesus. In the Seleucid period a new temple was begun on the ruins of the temple of Artemis; It was dedicated to the Phrygian goddess Cybele, who was identified with Artemis. Cybele was believed to have a special power of restoring life to the dead. Perhaps, this relates to Rev. 3:2 which urges the strengthening of that which is at the point of death. Sardis also was a commercial center for woolen goods. This is reflected in the garment imagery of Rev. 3:4-5, which refers to being clad in white, not in soiled garments.

When John wrote to Sardis, it was again a wealthy city, but without inner vitality. Spiritual decay had set in. Although the reputation of the city's past glory lingered, its people were degenerate and soft, preferring a life of ease and luxury and without zeal or vision for the future. The church there became a microcosm of its decayed social environment.

2. INTERRELATIONSHIPS WITHIN THE LETTER.

Interrelations are abundant between the cultural and historical background of this letter and its other constituent elements. Correlation is also found between words of consolation (promise, box 8) and preceding letter parts. In fact, every existing part of the letter somehow ties in to the cultural setting of the church.

As indicated in John 6:63, the Spirit gives life. The church in Sardis was largely devoid of that. Who would restore life? No mention is made of Cybele who had that reputation! No, it is the Christ figure (of 1:12ff.) who has the seven spirits, the symbol of spiritual life! The parts showing criticism, challenge, and confrontation (boxes #5, 6 and 7) relate to the same picture; but, they allude even more pointedly to the need to awaken. The church there must heed the memory of the two-time capture of a sleeping Sardis, taken by invasions that surprised them "like a thief." Most poignantly, the Armageddon passage (16:16) has the same setting of warning, namely that He comes "like a thief"; it also accents the blessedness of being awake and properly garbed, lest the nakedness be exposed.

The consolation (#8) found in the letter is threefold; one of the promises relates directly to the background (#2) of Sardis; the other two to other parts of the letter. The good news that the one who conquers will be clad in white plays on the reputation of Sardis' famous garment industry. Although the church there is described as "dead," there are still a few who have "unsoiled garments" and will wear the white garb of victory before God. Their names are written in the book of life. There is still hope, even for a moribund church, if it repents, awakes, and revives its works. For it still has a glimmer of life (even while "at the point of death"; see boxes 5 and P.S.). They can still rebound and find their names written in the Lamb's book of life.

3. CONTEMPORARY APPLICATIONS.

Goal: Churches and people like Sardis need renewed spiritual life. "Love is not love until it is given away." Jesus showed the way of sacrificial love for God's people (John 10:17; 15:12-13). Is our riches in the gospel and in material goods being shared to uplift the faith and life of God's other people? Preaching, teaching, and reaching to others with the word and the other blessings of life brings them new life; it also re-energizes God's called ones with the joy of giving that comes by responding to the Giver of <u>life</u> (the One "who has the seven <u>spirits</u> of God").

Threat: Empty boxes neatly labeled and stacked may give a picture of plenty even while hiding unfilled voids. Colorful spiritual balloons remain flat unless filled with the breath of life. Unread Bibles, unspoken encouragements, unprayed collects, unfed hungry ones, unloved people, and a neglected environment all are signs of stagnancy, an uncaring outlook, or a meaningless existence. A wake-up call is needed for those who have but don't use their spiritual resources and/or material goods to uplift God's people or to help make a better world. Faith requires fruits. Devoid of them, faith is dead.

Rescue. The reward for the steadfast and functioning Christian is heaven; John presents that promise in three ways. The faithful one will be: 1)dressed in white garments; 2)retained in the book of life; and, 3)commended to the Father and His angels at the judgment.

The **white garments** are the robes of victory (19:8, 14), duly washed in the blood of the Lamb (7:9, 13-14). These robes are reserved for those who have overcome in the struggles of life (6:11); and they will not be ashamed in the end (16:15).

The **book of life** includes the names of the elect who stand in the judgment and receive eternal life (20:12). Those who accept Jesus Christ will not have their names removed from this book (3:5). They are God's people and will dwell with Him in the New Jerusalem (21:4).

Jesus **commends the names** of those who have confessed Him before men. He will do so at the great white throne before the Father and His angels. He is faithful and will stand with those who have been awake to the leading of His Spirit. No one will snatch them out of Jesus' and the Father's hand (John 10:28-29).

4. CONCLUDING THOUGHT.

Jesus calls His church to confess Him before men by sharing His spirit and life with the world. Home and foreign missions give great opportunity for advancing the gospel of forgiveness and for improving others' quality of life through alleviating hunger, illness, and ignorance. When faith becomes smug and inactive, there is need for an infusion of God's Spirit and the reminder that "as you did it to one of the least of these my brethren, you did it to me" (Matt. 25:40). Failure to live out the faith subjects the complacent one to dire consequences. Faithful action receives the reward of the eternally secure life.

PHILADELPHIA

(REV. 3:7-13)

1. CULTURAL BACKGROUND.

Philadelphia was founded in 140 B.C. by Attalus II of Pergamum,[6] who was nicknamed "Philadelphos." It was a border city at the edge of Lydia and Phrygia and was located on the major highway that connected Europe to Asia in the East. Thus, it was perceived as a gateway city. Its purpose was to be a "missionary city" to bring Greek culture and language to the regions beyond. At John's time it had a "door of opportunity" to bring the gospel of Jesus Christ to outlying lands.

Philadelphia was at the edge of an extensive volcanic area whose soils were favorable for grape growing and wine making. The volcanoes made it an epicenter for earthquakes. When a major quake devastated it in 17 A.D., Emperor Tiberius provided generous aid to help them rebuild. The grateful populace responded by renaming its city Neocaesarea ("the new city of Caesar") in his honor.

In later years, when another major earthquake destroyed the city again, the then emperor, Vespasian, gave similar aid. Now the city was renamed Flavia, honoring this emperor's family name. Yet, always the name Philadelphia resurfaced as the city continued to honor the "brotherly love" which its founder, Attalus II, had for his older brother Eumenes. Whenever the frequent earth tremors came, the city dwellers would flee for safety from their vulnerable homes to the countryside; and then they would return when the after-shocks had ceased. Thus, they were always going out and coming back in again. Their enemies very likely taunted them with the suggestion that God didn't love them if they suffered so much. Eventually even they, "the synagogue of Satan," would see that God did love them!

The chief deity of the region was Dionysius, the god of wine, revered because the local economy depended on viticulture. The city had other temples also for other gods. Whenever the city chose to honor an exemplary citizen or benefactor, a pillar with his inscribed name was put into one of the temples. The extra pillar, in addition to honoring its namesake, also added stability to a temple, too often shaken by tremors.

2. INTERRELATIONSHIPS WITHIN THE LETTER.

The penchant for multiple names for the city (Philadelphia, Neocaesarea, Flavia; see box 2) is evident also in John's description of Jesus as the holy one, the true one, the one with the key of David (see box 3). Jesus is holy, that is, different from men; He is true in the sense of being genuine, the opposite of pretense and falsity. Having "the key of David," He has the authority to open and close, to admit or to exclude in the manner of Hezekiah's faithful steward, Eliakim (Isaiah 22:22). Thus, He has the key of Death and Hades (Rev. 1:18).

Jesus alone can open the door to God and to New Jerusalem (John 10:7). In the Jerusalem above there is only one temple; that temple is God and the Lamb, who dwell with God's people (Rev. 21:22; 22:3). This temple is eternal and unshakable. The faithful people in this temple will bear God's *name* on their foreheads (Rev. 22:4; see boxes 2, 8, and PS). The conquering saints, who had not denied Jesus' name (Rev. 3:8), also are granted a three-fold new name (of God, of New Jerusalem, and of Jesus; see Rev. 3:12 and boxes 4 and 8). Thus, they are God's own and dwell in the Jerusalem above.

The character of Jesus as "the holy and true" one is diametrically opposite to that of the synagogue of Satan and its lies (Rev. 3:7, 9; boxes 3 and 7). The church of Philadelphia, despite her "little power," had also been true, having kept Jesus' word, and hadn't denied His name. Thus, Philadelphia is one of only two of the seven churches for which there is no criticism or condemnation. These who have Jesus' word will be kept safe in the hour of trial (Rev. 3:8, 10; see boxes 4 and 8). That is their commendation and promise!

Despite their "little power," they have sufficient spiritual resources, having kept Jesus' word, to accept the challenge to "hold fast what you have, so that no one may seize your crown." (Rev. 3:8, 11; box 6). As Philadelphia had once been founded by secular leaders to serve as an "open door" to neighboring provinces for fostering the Hellenistic language and culture, so now she is in a position to be ambassador for the gospel of Jesus Christ. This open door no one is able to shut (Rev. 3:8). Their "little power," considering its divine source, is ample for seizing the opportunity of gospel outreach.

For the overcomers, there is the promise of never again having to flee from danger (going in and out of the city) because of recurrent earth tremors. Instead, they will be honored as pillars in the temple of God (box 8). That unique temple is in "New Jerusalem." There they experience blessedness in the presence of God and the Lamb.

3. CONTEMPORARY APPLICATIONS.

Goal:

- Hold fast what you have! Keep God's word as your spiritual resource! Let no one seize your crown!
- Endure patiently (despite threats of danger and doubt)!
- Keep an "open door" for sharing the gospel.

Threat:

- the "synagogue of Satan" that lies and deceives, that casts doubts about God's love when fears surface for one's life, safety, and property loss
- the temptation to waver and/or follow misleaders
- the excuse of having "little power" as validation for lack of spiritual zeal

Rescue:

- God's name is inscribed on you because you are His property.
- He'll keep you safe from "the hour of trial" that is coming on the whole world. (That includes judgment day; and also deliverance through such temporary trials as earthquakes, tornados, hurricanes, floods; and terrorist attacks or intimidation by religious adversaries or the powers that be.)
- He'll make the one who overcomes secure and will honor him by erecting him as a "pillar' in God's temple, which is His presence!
- In that temple, the believer will be with God and the Lamb with all the benefits of New Jerusalem (Rev. 21-22).

4. CONCLUDING THOUGHT.

Amid the tremors, trials, and tests of faith, the modern "Philadelphian" shares the hymnic prayer of James Montgomery:

> "In the hour of trial   Jesus plead for me
> Lest by base denial   I depart from Thee.
> When Thou seest me waver,   With a look recall
> Nor for fear or favor,   Suffer me to fall."

God's power and love sustains us in our weakness as we cast our care on Him. As we bear testimony to His name through fidelity in word and deed, even our spiritual detractors will have to take notice. Even more, we are heirs of the security and serenity of His abiding presence.

LAODICEA

(REV. 3:14-22)

1. CULTURAL BACKGROUND.

Laodicea was highly favored by royalty, location, and wealth. The Seleucid king Antiochus II had named the city after his wife Laodice. Located at the intersection of two major trade routes, commerce flourished. One imperial road ran south from the provincial capital Pergamum by way of Thyatira, Sardis, Philadelphia, and Laodicea to the Mediterranean. The other connected the Aegean Sea at Ephesus with Laodicea and the Anatolian plateau to the east. This promoted their banking interest and enabled a high volume of trade. The wealth of the city was legendary, reaching even the attention of Rome. Not only did the great orator Cicero use Laodicea's bank; but the city was so wealthy that she was able to rebuild without financial aid from Rome after the catastrophic earthquake of 60 A.D.

Besides money, manufacture and medicine added to her affluence. The surrounding region was admirably suited for raising sheep; their soft black wool supplied a profitable textile industry. Further fame came to Laodicea for her medical school and the products developed there for treating diseases of the ear and eye.

The affluent city had one major deficiency. The lukewarm (and mineral-tinged) water was not potable. For drinking purposes, they had to depend on an aqueduct to carry water from the springs of Denizli six miles to the south. By contrast, the hot springs of Hierapolis, six miles to the north were and are to this day, a famed health spa. However, by the time these waters flowed past Laodicea, they were no longer of medical value, nor were they drinkable.

Ironically, Smyrna, the only one of the seven churches not on both of the above referenced two roadways, was Laodicea's opposite. While the latter was rich in material things but spiritually poor, Smyrna was poor in material matters but rich spiritually. St. Paul's missionary umbrella had included Laodicea, as known from his letters (Col. 4:16). A large Jewish population of more than 7,500 adults was centered there. Also, the imperial cult was represented in Laodicea.

2. INTERRELATIONSHIPS WITHIN THE "LETTER."

The cultural background (box 2) is apparent in the criticism about being lukewarm (box 5). The affluence produced through woolen goods, medical products, and banking made for spiritual smugness. Resultantly box 6 reflects, perhaps surprisingly for her, the challenge to Laodicea to see her abject spiritual poverty. Ironically, she is in dire need of the *garments* of righteousness and spiritual *riches* and *healing*. She needs to repent and to accept the open door to God's offer of grace, as He stands at the door of opportunity and continues to knock. The consequences of refusal are devastating (box 7). Her current lukewarmness was so abhorrent that it would lead to vomiting. The reality is that her spirituality is wretched, poor, pitiable, blind, and exposed.

The promise to the repentant one (box 8) is that of dining and sitting with Jesus in glory in the splendor or the heavenly throne-room. That dramatically overshadows any benefit that emperor worship might provide to Laodicea (box 2). Rev. 20:4 and 22:2 (PS box) support the throne imagery and the vision of the delectable fruit in heaven.

3. CONTEMPORARY APPLICATIONS.

Goal:
- Go to the "Amen," the certified Savior, the one who is faithful and true. He both promises and provides spiritual gold, the garments of righteousness, and the salve of forgiveness and peace.
- Discover the purchase price as that of simply and humbly opening the door to His invitation and fellowship.

- Find sufficiency and salvation in worship at His throne, knowing that grace is God's gift.

Threat:
- being smug and self-satisfied with one's own achievements and resources
- thinking that material prosperity is a true sign of God's favor
- being blind to our spiritual poverty and our pitiable condition before the "Amen," the faithful and true one, as we assert our own relative merits (Our merits do not cover our sins, and are as unacceptable to the divine taste buds as the lukewarm water that flowed by their city was to the Laodiceans.)

Rescue: Jesus knocks on the door of our heart and invites us to accept His fellowship and His lordship. That involves receiving and sharing with others the blessings of enthronement with Him in glory and of dining with Him there from the bounties of His grace. His grace includes the *gold* of eternal riches in heaven, the *garments* of righteousness which hide our shame, and the healing *salve* which restores correct vision before the one who, as "the beginning of God's creation," overshadows even emperors.

4. CONCLUDING THOUGHT.

The closing promise to the church of Laodicea focuses the basic issue of the book of Revelation: **the throne!** Who really rules our life? Is it an earthly king? Or is it the King of kings?

The one who conquers, who remains faithful to Jesus unto death, the Amen, the true witness, will be welcomed to the heavenly throne room. As Jesus Himself conquered and was raised to sit with the Father on His throne, so those who receive His grace and walk in His way will also be raised and receive enthronement. The throne of worldly potentates, with its scant and fleeting rewards, pales in comparison!

John's concluding admonition, "hear what the Spirit says to the churches," given here a seventh and last time, has universal application. The messages to these historic seven churches provide an aggregate word for the church of all time. They warn against the dangers of:

- losing the first love (Ephesus)
- reluctance to bear the Christian cross (Smyrna)
- tolerating doctrinal compromise (Pergamum)
- tolerating moral laxity (Thyatira)
- being spiritually asleep (Sardis)
- having only slight spiritual strength (Philadelphia)
- feeling smug and self-sufficient (Laodicea)

In regard to each of these dangers, the composite word of promise and consolation to the churches, given in its rich variety, gives ample encouragement to the saints to persevere to the moment of the summons from heaven's throne.

_____

[1]This was at the time that Jesus began His public ministry.

[2] Polycarp is the model here for unflinching faithfulness and piety even in the face of death. To read the dramatic and inspiring account of his martyrdom, refer to Edgar Goodspeed's The Apostolic Fathers: an American Translation, "The Martyrdom of Polycarp." New York: Harper and Brothers, 1950, pages 245-256.

[3]Daniel 10:6 has similar depiction of the angel there.

[4]Barclay,   Letters to the Seven Churches.   Philadelphia: Westminster Press, 1957, p. 79.

[5]Ibid.

[6]Ibid., p. 94.

CHAPTER V

THE UNHOLY THREE (REV. 12-13)

Revelation 12-14 introduces the second half of Revelation by introducing with utter clarity the villain of the book, his collaborators, and the forecast of their dismal and deserved demise. Satan is the ultimate villain as he opposes the Lamb, Christ. Satan's prime associates who serve as an attack force in John's vision are described as "the beast out of the sea" and "the beast out of the earth" in chapter 13. The latter two morph into Babylon in chapter 14 and following. Those who have fallen for Babylon's wiles are described as having "the mark of the beast" (666) in chapters 13-16. The sorry fate of each of these anti-Christian forces is depicted in subsequent chapters. For those with the beast's mark, chapters 15-16 tell their tale of woe; chapters 17-19, for Harlot Babylon and the two beasts; and chapter 20, for the dragon.

In chapter 12 the woman and the dragon are described as signs, as larger than life figures. In verses 1-6 the woman is depicted as bearing the child who thwarted the dragon's deadly designs; verses 7-12 offer a glimpse into heaven's expulsion of the dragon's forces at the hand of Michael and his angels; verses 13-17 depict the deliverance of the woman from the dragon. Each segment leads up to the ultimate victory of God and His people, celebrated in chapter 14.

The first scene lists the first of Revelation's "signs," a significant event. It sheds light on the woman's role as carrier of the promise. She represents the global and timeless community of faith that includes both the believers of the Old Testament era and the church of the New Testament age. From the very beginning the promise was given that despite the enmity of the serpent (Satan), the woman and her offspring would overcome (Gen. 3:15). The woman is clothed with light (sun, moon, and stars) "from head to toe," befitting her role as the one to whom and for whom "the Light of the World" (John 8 and 9) would and did come.

THE CHILD TRIUMPHS

The second sign (v. 3) features her opponent, the dragon; that's not just any dragon, but one that is great and red. Red signifies his murderous penchant for blood. His *heads* signal his authority and influence; the *horns*, his power; the *diadems*, the claim of his rule over the world (compare 13:1-2, where the dragon invests the beast with his "weaponry"). Rev.12:4-5 dramatizes the dragon's destructive power by suggesting that the twitch of his tail can dislodge a third of the stars; also, it reveals his murderous intent (as in John 8:40-44) against the woman's child, God's Son! Verse 5 identifies this child as the Messiah (in referring to Psalm 2:9 which describes the ideal future king thusly). Herod had failed to cut short Jesus' mission despite the slaughter of other babes at Bethlehem. The role of Pilate and chief priests in Jerusalem at the crucifixion of Jesus more than thirty years later only served as a fulcrum that moved the redemptive plan of God toward its goal.

In one sentence John compressed the story of Jesus from incarnation to ascension (v. 5). In short, he shows that Jesus fulfilled the mission on which God sent Him, overcoming the deadly schemes of the devil. God rewarded the child's (Jesus') fidelity by sharing His throne in heaven (v. 5). As the Apostles' Creed states, "from thence He will come to judge." That throne makes all other thrones appear powerless (including especially those of abusive emperors such as Domitian and of Satan himself, the so-called "ruler of this world").

As for the "woman" (God's faithful people), they too escape the dragon as they find shelter in the wilderness (much as young David had when he fled King Saul's darts). This shelter will sustain them for their full earthly sojourn (1260 days, 3½ years, the symbolic time until Jesus' return to usher in "the new heavens and the new earth"). And yes, the wilderness period represents the full time between Jesus' earthly ministry and His return as Judge.

THE WAR IN HEAVEN

The second scene of chapter 12 pictures how the dragon entered human history (vv. 7-12). The rebellious Satan and his angels had been thrown out of heaven (see also Jude 6). Michael, the defender of

God's people (Daniel 10:13-21), together with his angels, had defeated the ancient serpent (Gen. 3), who is also called "the devil and Satan, the deceiver of the whole world" (v. 9). As a result, the *head*ship, the power (*horn*), and the kingdom (*crown*) surely and securely are that of God and Christ (v. 10). Satan's accusations and condemnations of the faithful are now groundless as the Lamb has paid the wages of sin and death, and has overcome both, as signaled by His own atoning death, resurrection, and ascension. Thus, God's faithful people are rescued by the redemptive blood of the Lamb and by their fidelity in word and deed "even unto death" (v. 11 and 2:10). But eternal vigilance is still required as the devil's wrathful aggression continues against mankind until the end of history (v. 12, and 1 Peter 5:8). Because of the dragon's furor, earthlings will continue amid the woe he generates. While two of the three woes (see 8:13) are depicted as past (in 9:12 and 11:14), the final woe will cease at the final judgment when the devil and his henchmen are "thrown into the lake of fire and brimstone" (Rev. 20:10).

Having lost the battle against the Messiah, God's Son, and having been excluded from heaven by Michael and the "good angels," the devil is skating on thin ice. One may ask, "Why doesn't he quit?" Could it be that the great deceiver (v. 9) has also deceived himself with the idea that he can gain a measure of satisfaction by destroying many of God's people? The good news is that his time is short (v. 12) and that God and Michael's angels have done and will do their part to seek and preserve the lost (Luke 19:10).

THE WOMAN FINDS SECURITY

Scene three shows the dragon in hot pursuit of the woman (the community of the redeemed). However, just as Israel was borne "on eagles' wings" (Exod. 19:4) through the wilderness to the Lord's presence at Mount Sinai, so it is with the church in her wilderness trek. She, too, will be sustained "for a time, times, and a half" (v. 14, the symbolic 3½ years of the church's "wilderness" life preceding the Lord's return). Nevertheless, the attack from the dragon's mouth continues (v. 15) as he pours out his venom of malicious lies and persecution against the woman (the church) and seeks to drown out her life with a flood of false doctrine and destructive actions. Examples of how this still happens through misleaders and authority figures, both religious and secular (ravenous wolves in sheep's clothing), could be multiplied.

Even as Satan used Pharaoh's army to trap Israel at the sea, and as God's miracle at the same sea intervened in their behalf (Exod. 14 and 15), so God's power will support the church till the end of time so that "not even the gates of Hades will prevail against it" (Matt. 16:18). Even though the angry thrice-foiled dragon continues his attack on the latter-day "offspring" of the woman, he knows that his cause is shaky. "He stood on the *sand* of the sea" (v. 17). Confidently, the woman's offspring gains strength as she sings, "On Christ the solid *rock* I stand; all other ground is sinking sand." Although "the ruler of this world is cast out" (John 12:31) and bound and thrown into the bottomless pit (Rev. 20:1-3), he hasn't given up yet. His destructive quest for the souls of men continues through intermediaries. Chapter 13 will give insight into how the devil used human authorities and agencies to go to bat for him against the churches of Asia to which John wrote.

THE DEVIL'S DEADLY DUO

In chapter 13 the beast and the "false prophet" complete the counterfeit trinity anchored by Satan. These two beasts represent Satan's collaborators for enacting his dire designs. Chapter 12 ends with the dragon knocked down, but not out just yet, as he stands on the unstable sand of the sea. In contrast, we will find the victorious Lamb portrayed in Rev. 14:1 as standing on the solid rock of the glorious Mount Zion. These two portraits frame the chapter that introduces the beastly pair.

THE FIRST BEAST

Standing at the edge of his sea of futility, the dragon welcomes the beast out of the sea (13:1). This is a symbolic reference to the emissaries who bring the imperial decrees ashore in Asia. The relationship of the two is obvious. Each is characterized by heads, horns, and diadems in multiples of ten or seven. Different from his satanic sponsor, this beast sports his diadems on his horns, symbolizing the use of power to exercise his brutalities. The dragon had worn his diadems on his heads, signifying his ambition for domination and control. Even so, their ambition is fused in their blasphemous commitment to idolatry against the holy trinity. The name on the beast's head reflects the worship of Caesar, which dated back to the first Roman emperor. That worship was now seriously enforced at John's time, forcing him to exile on the isle of Patmos in the 90's during the reign of Domitian. With renewed force the emperor insisted on being worshipped as "Lord and God" (*Dominus et Deus*).

Like the vision in Daniel 7, the beast has the nimbleness of a leopard, the brute strength of a bear, and the ferocity of a roaring lion (1 Peter. 5:8), and ten horns! The beast uses all of these for its deadly deeds.

The mortal head wound, now healed (v. 3), appears to be a reference to Emperor Nero. Decades earlier he had ordered the cruel slaughter of Christians in Rome after he burned the city, only to commit suicide himself years later. One legend held that Nero hadn't actually died, but had fled to Parthia and one day would return at the head of the feared Parthian army to wreak revenge on Rome. At any rate, the vindictive *spirit* of Nero would return, as it had in the person of Emperor Domitian, who persecuted John and the churches of Asia.

Worship of the emperor was common in the cities to which John wrote from exile (Rev. 2-3); and many of them contained temples dedicated to the emperor and other Greco-Roman deities. Such worship pleased Satan (the dragon) and was allowed to continue for a symbolic 42 months. These 3½ years depict not only the age of John but also the whole age of the church (in her wilderness trek until the Lord brings her into her heavenly promised land). Was there ever an age when the suffering caused by power-mongers wasn't present somewhere?

The saints (those whose anchor is in heaven, vv.6-7) are subjected to both religious blasphemy against their God and to physical torment. The passive verbs of verse 7 suggest that despite the evil of the beast, God is still in charge and will reward the saints' fidelity amid their adversity. In contrast to these faithful ones (whose names are in the Lamb's book of life), those whose life is dominated by earthly pursuits would cave in to the beast and worship it. This seemed to be universal practice (as signaled by the cosmic four-fold listing of tribe, people, tongue, and nation, v. 8).

The call for the endurance of the saints (vv. 9-10) is a solemn one, as signaled by the formula "If anyone has an ear, let him hear" (also found seven times in the letters to the seven churches of chapters 2-3). That call recognizes the reality of suffering and cross-bearing for the Christian (Matt. 16:24-27). Nevertheless, there is also some consolation in the reminder of the dire future fate of the contemporary violent men and institutions. God is still in charge! The reward for the Christian's perseverance is the same as that promised to the church of Smyrna; they were assured, "Be faithful unto death, and I will give you the crown of life" (2:10). That reassurance will be further heightened in Rev. 14, which also presents a "call for perseverance" in 14:12ff.

THE SECOND BEAST

If the beast out of the sea is Mr. Outside, the beast out of the land is Mr. Inside. They work in tandem, "two peas in a pod." The marine beast represents imperial Rome with her mandate that all citizens must comply with the annual loyalty pledge to the empire and its leader. By giving the pinch of incense and verbally honoring the emperor as "Lord and God," Rome sought to receive the unification and spiritual support of her diverse far-flung empire that rimmed the Mediterranean Sea.

However, she needed the support of the religious and civil leaders in the various provincial areas to enforce this effort. That role is attributed to "the beast out of the land." It represented the priests, philosophers, orators, and the various political leaders who would propagandize in behalf of Rome and mete out penalties to harass non-compliant ones. The saints of the seven churches were bruised severely by the two "horns" of this beast.

This beast is a deceiving fraud as it had the innocent appearance of a lamb, an obvious parody on the Lamb that was slain (5:9), whom the Christians worshipped. It mirrors the proverbial "wolves in sheep's clothing," described by Jesus as "false prophets" (Matt. 7:15). While outwardly taking on the appearance of a respected community leader, its acts were in synch with the murderous dragon and the beast out of the sea. The issue was clearly one of worship (v. 12)! Earthly-minded people were seduced or forced to worship the emperor (the first beast). The spirit of Nero ("whose mortal wound was healed," symbolically understood) was alive and well in Domitian. John warns "those who dwell in heaven" (v. 6) of the tricks used to deceive and persuade their opponents, "those who dwell on earth" (v. 14). Evidence exists that images were constructed of the emperor in local settings; they had bodily vents and hidden mechanisms which could cause the emission of "breath" (vapor or smoke) and even enable ventriloquism in behalf of the emperor's image. All of this was to beguile the gullible citizenry. Not surprisingly, then, this beast is later consistently identified as "the false prophet" (in Rev. 16:3; 19:20; and 20:10).

This beast confronted all levels of society (small and great, rich and poor, free and slave; v. 16). Christians were at risk of physical harm, even death, or economic sanctions for refusal to worship in this false manner. A mark on the forehead or the right hand would free the emperor-worshippers from discrimination in the market place. The saints (the symbolic 144,000 of Rev. 7:3) while not spared in this way, however, would be spared by God in a far superior way. In Rev. 7:3 we see that they receive God's seal on their foreheads! This identified them as God's own whose names are to be found in the Lamb's book of life! To this day those who receive Christian baptism bear the identity of God's own children! Their seal separates them out in life and in worship from those who would bear the mark (or I.D.) of the beast.

THE MARK OF THE BEAST

Given that much of the book's comfort, as well as warnings are couched in cryptic language, Rev. 13:18 is no exception. It is one of the most puzzling verses of the Apocalypse. Wisdom is required (here and in Rev. 17:9, where the "seven hills" more clearly identify Rome as the problem of the book)! The number 666 is a human number. Symbolically, it can be explained as the symbol for the ultimate evil. If six signifies evil, its three-fold repetition gives emphasis to that by making it obvious and unmistakable . Six falls short of the perfect number seven, and signifies evil or sin. While God is perfect (Matt. 5:48), the emperor is not! Far from it! Since 666 is described as a human number, many have sought to connect it with a specific person, often in creative or even ludicrous ways. Probably none of the historic identifications for this person fits better than the name of Nero. This can be argued both on the basis of the historic context of the book and on the basis of numeric symbolism.

Gerhard Krodel[1] follows the lead of other commentators in stating that the Hebrew spelling for Emperor Nero, *Neron Caesar,* would be written as follows: "*nron qsr* (*nun*=50 + *resh*=200 + *waw*=6 + *nun*=50 + *qoph*=100 + *samekh*=60 +*resh*=200)." The sum of these numeric equivalents is 666. This identification also accounts for the variant reading of the Western text manuscript which has 616 instead of 666. The Latin form for "*Neron*" would drop the final "n" (*nun*), accounting for the 50 subtracted from the 666. Also, the numeric value for the word "beast," (*therion*) in Greek, is 666 when using Hebrew letters.[2] None of the many other attempts at identifying a human villain with the number 666 can satisfy both the text and its variant reading. The reference to the mortal wound that was healed (13:3) lends further support for allusion to the *Nero redivivus* theory.

To be sure, the idolatry rampant at John's time, newly enforced in Domitian's reign as the ultimate evil, is characterized by the symbolic meaning of the number six (and 666!). Does not also the Decalogue begin with the command, "Thou shall have no other gods before me?" The Judeo-Christian heritage places the highest premium on the unique role of God as creator, redeemer, sanctifier, and preserver! That description certainly does not fit the emperor, or any other deity for that matter!

Finally, as Bruce Metzger says,[3] "It is always a choice between the power that operates through *inflicting* suffering, that is, the power of the beast, and the power that operates through *accepting* suffering, namely, the power of the Lamb." While the destructive efforts of the "counterfeit trinity" causes much temporal suffering and grief, John always comes back to his readers with the consoling message of hope for the future enduring bliss that is the lot of the persevering saints. For a glimpse of that, we continue with John's next chapter.

[1]Revelation, Augsburg Commentary. Minneapolis: Augsburg Publishing Co., 1989, p. 259.
[2]Ibid.

[3]Breaking the Code. Nashville: Abingdon Press, 1993, p. 77.

CHAPTER VI

THE SAINTS' VICTORY

There is a dramatic mood shift to one of triumph for the persevering saints as the reader enters chapter 14. After being confronted by the antagonistic ungodly trio and a depressing glimpse of earthly realities in the preceding two chapters, the joyous prospect of heaven comes into view. Three distinct scenes are depicted, all dealing with either the eternal reward of the saints or the deserved punishment of their adversaries. The Greek verb "*I saw*" in verses 1, 6, and 14 introduces the three sections of the chapter.

JOY ON MOUNT ZION

The presence of the 144,000 on Mt. Zion reflects the future bliss that awaits the church militant. She is introduced in Rev. 7:1-8 as sealed and protected against the ravages of time. Hebrews 12:22-24 describes such a festal gathering on Mt. Zion in similar terms. Here the redeemed are assembled around the Lamb, Who stands on the solid bedrock of the idealized Mt. Zion, in utter contrast to the dragon, who stood on the sea's shifting sand (12:17). In contradistinction to those bearing the *mark* of the beast, those on Mt. Zion have the *name* of the Lamb and the Father inscribed on their foreheads. They are God's treasure trove. They, and they only, can sing the new song, first surfaced in Rev. 5:9-10. It is the reward for their spiritual virginity (*parthenoi,* 14:4). Their "chastity" consists of resisting the allurements of "women" (read: the idolatrous harlot Babylon of Rev. 17), of following the leading of the Lamb, and of offering themselves as "first fruits" for God (14:4-5). The "lie" of Babylon which they resisted is a reference to the emperor's insistence that he be worshiped as "Lord and God." The Father and the Lamb merit worship, but certainly not Domitian or any other human figure.

THREE URGENT MESSAGES

The pattern of Rev. 11:12 is here repeated. After the faithful there are depicted as going up to heaven in a cloud, the next verse returns to an earthly scene that signals God's judgment. Similarly, here after viewing the blessedness of the saints in glory, John brings the reader back to the events on earth that precede the judgment at the second coming. The three angels of verses 6, 8, and 9 have a single purpose, namely to warn men of the coming judgment and to call them to repentance.

The first angelic call (Rev. 14:6-7) focuses on universal outreach, signaled by the cosmic four-fold reference to nation, tribe, tongue, and people. The worship of all is to center on the unique God, creator of all humanity. Along similar lines, the first four trumpets of #8:7-12 showed Him as sovereign over all of the four-fold natural world (heaven and earth, sea and inland waters).

The second angel (v. 8) prophetically announced the fall of Babylon as accomplished fact. This is the first strong clue in Revelation who the immediate threat to John's churches is. It will remain for a later chapter to further clarify that Babylon refers to the power structures of Rome, the empire that radiated forth from the seven hills (17:9). Indeed, the corrupt empire would fall a few centuries later. In a larger sense, Babylon's fate exemplified that of all evil power structures. Their destiny is one of eventual doom.

The third angel (vv. 9-11) concludes the triad of judgment calls with a most severe warning. Those who persist in the seductive ways of the "beast" and carry its mark of identity will be doomed to "the wine of God's wrath" (v. 10f.). John minces no words here as he refers to the eternal fire and brimstone usually associated with hell. Some self-made interpreters recoil at the thought that this could happen "in the presence of the holy angels . . . and of the Lamb." One need only review the judgment scene in Matthew 25:41 to see that John is merely echoing the very thought of Jesus Himself.

THE CALL FOR ENDURANCE

There is debate among scholars whether the call for endurance pertains to the preceding or to the succeeding section of this chapter. The flow of John's message would suggest that it flows both forward and backward. It is foreshadowed in 13:10 by the call there to endure the abuse of the beast(s). Here in 14:12, the call comes within a much more comforting context. There had already been the vision of heavenly bliss for those who were identified with the name of the Father and the Lamb. This was followed by three assurances that the wicked or the wavering ones would suffer dire eternal consequences if they had the beast's mark. The second endurance call is reinforced by a trio of voices that sharpen the focus of 14:1-11.

THREE VOICES FROM HEAVEN

The first voice from God (heaven) in this triad (14:13, 15, and 18) is also the first beatitude since Rev. 1:3, which blessed the one who read, heard, and kept the book's message. The blessing of 14:13 gives the content to the earlier promise. "Blessed are the dead who die in the Lord" is the heart and soul of the gospel. It is the blessed assurance that powers the Christian's walk in the way of the Lamb. The message of this voice is further supported by the voices of the two scenes of harvest, or judgment, that follow.

The two other voices from heaven trigger the final harvest, depicted in two separate scenes (vv. 14-20). In each case an "angel" is poised for action before the command from heaven came for reaping the ripened harvest. The reaper swings his sickle into action at the call of the voice. Regarding the first harvest scene (vv. 14-16), some see this as a reference to the general judgment of all. If that is the intent of the writer, it underscores the fact that God is in charge and will judge everyone in the end. That is a strong call to endurance in the faith. On the other hand, if it refers only to "bringing in the sheaves," a harvest of the righteous, it serves as a reassurance of the message of the beatitude (in 14:13) for the comfort of the faithful.

The third voice in the series leaves no doubt regarding the scope of that harvest. "The great winepress of the wrath of God" clearly targets and squishes the worshipers of the beast, who then must "drink the wine of God's wrath" (14:10). In a complete turnabout, the One who "suffered outside the gate" (Jesus, see Hebrews 13:12) and trod the winepress alone (Isaiah 63:3; Joel 3:13) to ransom men for God (Rev. 5:9), now is the *agent* for judgment "outside the city" (v. 20). The judgment of the vintage is all-inclusive, as denoted by the flow of "the blood" of the grapes for 1,600 stadia. As explained in the chapter on symbolism, the *meaning* of the number is key here. The square of 4 is 16; multiplied by the square of 10, it yields 1,600. Four symbolizes the things on earth (as opposed to heavenly things); ten is the number of completeness. So, the multiplication of these numeric symbols reinforces the fact that all earthlings who do not follow the Lamb are implicated in the judgment.

This is the same message that is restated more simply in Rev. 20:12-15. For the significance of the "horse's bridle," see the comment on #14:20 in the chapter on symbolism. As stated there, it connects with the horse's rider [Jesus], whose robe "is dipped in blood" (19:11-13). Why otherwise would a horse be in a winepress, unless for making a symbolic point? As Rev. 1:7 states, "All tribes of the earth will wail on account of" the One "coming with the clouds." The judgment is no matter to trifle with. By the same token, Jesus, the rider on the white horse, by treading the winepress alone, also ransomed men for God at the expense of His blood!

THE SEALED SAINTS

To appreciate more fully the joy of the redeemed who stand on Mt. Zion with the Lamb and who have His and the Father's names on their foreheads, it is well to return to the "sealing" scene of chapter seven. Indeed, the preservation of the faithful from the dragon and his deadly duo of cohorts depicted in Rev. 12-13 is both amazing and gratifying. Indeed, the saints are rescued not only from the assaults of their spiritual and human enemies, but also are shielded from destruction amid the slings of a fallen natural world.

After the opening of the horrific sixth seal in Rev. 6, the reader might expect that the four angels who had the "power to harm earth and sea"(7:2) would indeed release the four winds. It didn't happen.

Instead, the four angels at the earth's four corners prevent the four winds from devastating the redeemed. (Four is the digit of geographic universality in the Apocalypse.) Despite the cross-bearing that Christians will encounter as faithful witnesses to the Lamb, they will not be overwhelmed by it (7:1-3). They will have the divine protection that enables their endurance through the promises and provisions God affords them. After all, they are His beloved ones, bearing His spiritual seal on their foreheads. In Holy Scripture, the seal on the forehead indicates protection and ownership. They are God's; and as 1 John 4:4 says, "He who is in you is greater than he who is in the world." The Lamb will shepherd His spiritual sheep (Rev. 7:17) and will clip the dragon's fangs. Even so, the protection doesn't ward off all physical harm. It is spiritual. (Note: the witnesses in chapter 11 were killed before they later ascended to heaven.)

THE 144,000

The people of God are identified by the numeral 144,000. As with most numbers in Revelation, it is a symbolic numeral. The square of twelve (which designates the faithful flock) multiplied by the cube of ten (the number of completeness) equals 144,000. It includes all the faithful of any and all ages during the time up to the Lord's return as Judge. In no way is this figure to be interpreted literally, nor does it benefit only literal Jews, as some have argued. Salvation is not for a limited number only.

The inclusion and selection of the twelve tribal names has led to considerable discussion. While the number of tribes remains intact throughout Scripture, the names of the titular heads vary in meaningful ways in various contexts. They key can be found along the lines of theological points. Here, Judah (the fourth-born of Jacob) is listed first; it is the tribe through which the Messiah Jesus came. Thus, it has a unique role. The names of Dan and Ephraim, two of the twelve tribes receiving lands at Joshua's time, are omitted for good reason. In their territories were the shrines of Dan and Bethel, centers of idolatry in the land of ancient Israel. What a discrete move by John in his book which is dedicated to preserve and encourage the fidelity of the saints who are confronted with the lures of idolatry! Instead of these two,

Joseph (rather than Ephraim) is paired with his son Manasseh; and Levi, whose tribe received no land holdings, completes the twelve in place of Dan. Even as the twelve tribes represent the people of God in the Old Testament, so the twelve apostles were foundational for the church of the New Testament age. The 144,000 reflects not only Jewish believers, but includes also Gentiles, "the Israel of God" (Gal. 6:16). It represents the church militant in her life under the cross of Christ.

THE NUMBERLESS THRONG

The second vision (7:9-17) is of the church triumphant. It is parallel to the first vision in that it refers to the same people, distinguished only by time and location. All segments of humanity are represented (nations, tribes, peoples, and tongues, the four-fold universal grouping). The unnumbered multitude stands before the throne of God and the Lamb adorned with white robes and palm branches, symbols of victory and salvation. Unlike the first vision which found the redeemed surrounded by danger, here they are found secure and jubilant as they praise God and the Lamb. All the company of heaven (angels, elders, and living creatures) join in the blissful worship.

Verses 14 to 17 contain two paradoxes. They answer two questions: 1) What qualifies the victors? and, 2) What is heaven like? The qualification for celebrating the presence of holy God is simply wearing the robes made white by the blood of the Lamb. The robes of victory are His gift. White, the symbolic color of both victory and purity, is attained through the redemptive ministry of the Lamb of God whose shed blood on Calvary takes away the sins of the world (John 1:29). Thus, the church sings, "Behold a host arrayed in white!" They have endured the great tribulation of their earthly sojourn in which they took up the cross, following the Lamb! Of course, washing with blood doesn't result in a literal whiteness. The symbolic and spiritual meaning here is obvious!

The second paradox serves the second question: "What is heaven like?" In another amazing tour de force the Lamb becomes a shepherd. John 10 (Jesus as the Good Shepherd) and Psalm 23 ("the Shepherd Psalm") have prepared the reader well for this paradox. The

Lamb not only is the means for salvation, but also He will be present in "the realms of glory" with those dressed in white. These are among the most consoling and uplifting scenes in all of Scripture. They serve as inspiration for the church militant as she yearns to be the church triumphant. To be with God and to serve Him in His temple (v. 15) is to be in heaven. While there is no physical temple in heaven (Rev. 21:22), the reader understands that the temple and the tabernacle pictures in Scripture generally pertain to God's spiritual presence among His people. In that sense, He is always with His flock. This is their constant basis for support, strength, hope, and joy. In the presence of the Lamb at heaven's throne there will be no more hardships such as those caused by hunger and thirst, scorching heat, or the tears of grief and pain (vv. 16-17). These words of encouragement fortify the "sealed" until they reach and realize the fullness of joy at the celestial throne.

OTHER SCENES OF HOPE

John deals forthrightly with life's realities. In so doing, he also repeatedly echoes the words of Jesus, "I have said this to you, that in Me you may have peace. In the world you have tribulation; but be of good cheer, I have overcome the world." (John 16:33) Similarly, Paul and Barnabas had reminded the Christians of Galatia that "through many tribulations we must enter the kingdom of God." (Acts 14:22)

Despite the challenges that secular governments and society in general thrust upon the Lamb's disciples, John regularly interjects words of promise and hope throughout the Apocalypse. Without attempting a complete listing, we offer a few of the more obvious examples in Rev. 2-3; 5:1-14; 11:15-19; and chapters 19-22.

In the letters to the seven churches (Rev. 2-3), John consistently offers words of promise and hope. These are appropriate to each of the individual churches in keeping with the challenges they face in their local settings, as described in the above chapter that deals with the seven churches of Asia.

In the frustrating scene at the start of Rev. 5, where no one was able to open the scroll's seven seals which brought John to weep bitterly, the Lamb comes to the rescue. The scroll contained the plan for human history. Was there any meaning and purpose for life? The answer is provided as one of the elders around the throne in heaven points John to the Lion of the tribe of Judah, the root of David (Genesis 49:9; Isaiah 11:1, 10). Here in another of the great paradoxes of the Apocalypse, the Lion morphs into the Lamb. Both the lion and the aura of King David suggest conquering might. However, the Lamb figure portrays something very different, sacrificial love! Through His gentle spirit of submission to the Father's plan, the Suffering Servant (Isaiah 53:5), standing although slain, saved man's destiny! By His blood He "ransomed men for God" and "made them a kingdom" (5:5-10). Instead of a David-like warrior who would ward off the Roman oppression, the Lamb rode into Jerusalem on a donkey, symbol of peace and humility. He alone was found worthy to open the future for mankind. His atoning sacrifice is cause for jubilation by the whole company of heaven, which now can sing a new song, the song of redemption (5:9-14).

Another moment for celebration in Revelation is found in the aftermath of the first six trumpets in the interlude of chapters 10-11. Despite the suffering of the witnesses at the hands of their persecutors, they ascend to heaven in the sight of their foes (11:12). Then follows the seventh trumpet with the announcement that "the kingdom of the world has become the kingdom of our Lord and His Christ, and He shall reign forever and ever" (11:15). It is a time "for rewarding those who fear thy name, both small and great, and for destroying the destroyers of the earth" (v. 18). The celebration culminates with the full revelation of God's presence in heaven. Finally, the complete significance of the temple and the ark of the covenant come into view amid the signs of theophany (lightning, thunder, earthquake, and hail, v. 19).

The climax of "the revelation of Jesus Christ" (Rev. 1:1) is reserved for the closing chapters of the book (#19-22). These jubilant scenes come close on the heels of the dramatic vision of the fall of Babylon in chapter 18. Babylon is the first century re-incarnation of the sin against the first commandment: idolatry. The Almighty and the Lamb will triumph completely in God's good time, at the end of world history. The victory scenes are presented in two ways: by dramatic portraits of the final judgment, and by a vision of the glories of heaven.

The judgment scenes show God's final defeat and disposal of the enemies listed in the book. They include: 1) Babylon and those who bear the mark of the beast and worship its image (Rev. 16-18); 2) The beast and false prophet (Rev. 19); and, 3) the dragon, Satan (Rev. 20). The latter context includes the consoling interlude of the millennial reign of the souls of those who died in the Lord. These scenes will be developed in the next chapter.

The magnificent glories of heaven, which transcend human powers of comprehension, are the subject of later chapters of this book also. They will be developed in terms of two sets of clashing symbols that find their culmination at the end of Revelation. These are: first, *the New Jerusalem* "coming down out of heaven" (21:2) versus Babylon, "thrown down with violence" (18:21), a tale of two cities; and second, the marriage of *the bride* versus the fate of the harlot, a tale of two women.

CHAPTER VII

THE MILLENNIUM AND ARMAGEDDON

Life is lived on two levels---the present and the future, with the past as prologue. Faith, the spark of life, likewise operates on both levels. We need faith in the present to give us courage, and in the future to give us hope. It is within this framework that Revelation 20 deals with two significant concepts of the Revelation of Jesus Christ, the millennium and Armageddon (the latter so designated in Rev. 16:16).

The concept of the *millennium* addresses the present reward of those who have died in the Lord, or will die before His second coming. *Armageddon*, on the other hand, is one of several portraitures in Revelation of that moment in time when the Lord returns visibly to usher in the glorious future of the faithful of all ages and to separate out the rest.

THE MILLENNIUM

The concept of the millennium is introduced in six tightly clustered verses, Rev. 20:2-7. It is a subject much debated in regard to its temporal length and the nature of the "reign" of the "blessed" ones. A careful reading of these verses within the context of the rest of Holy Scripture will reveal the blessedness of the faithful departed. When we briefly deal with several questions frequently raised, we provide commentary with answers consistent with the whole of Scripture. We also indicate how the literalistic view of the 1,000 years is misleading and contrary to the teaching of Jesus and His N. T. witnesses. So then, let us proceed to the questions raised by Rev. 20:1-7. Among the most obvious questions are the following.

1. When and how do the binding and loosing of Satan occur?
2. How long is the millennium and when is it?
3. What is the nature of the enthronement and reign?
4. Who will sit on thrones and reign with Christ?

5. Who are "the rest of the dead"?
6. What is "the first resurrection" and "the second death"?
7. How does the millennium relate to Armageddon?

BINDING AND LOOSING

The focus here is on the arch-enemy of Christ. He is described in Rev. 20:2 by the same four names by which he is introduced in 12:9. There he is called the dragon (thrown out of heaven), the ancient serpent (who deceived Eve, Gen. 3), the devil, and Satan. His binding took place during Jesus' earthly sojourn (from the incarnation to His ascension), briefly delineated in Rev. 12:5. Through His ministry, death, resurrection, and ascension Jesus manifested the kingdom of God as He overcame Satan's every temptation and every claim. The four evangelists allude to this binding of Satan (Mark 3:27; Matt. 12:29; Luke 11:21f., and John 12:20-32). The synoptic Gospels refer to the binding of the strong man (Satan) by the one stronger (Jesus) than he. The Fourth Gospel gives additional clarity to this picture in connection with the Greeks' coming to Jesus. The Lord there (John 12:31-32), while meditating on His coming crucifixion and resurrection, declares that "now shall the ruler of this world be cast out; and I, when I am lifted up from the earth, will draw all men to myself." No longer would Satan be able to blind the nations and keep them from coming to Christ. By His crucifixion, resurrection, and ascension Jesus clearly manifested the Father's will that all men be saved, both Jew and Gentile! He is able to overcome Satan's tricks and attacks on Christians because "He who is in you is greater than he who is in the world" (1 John 4:4).

So, the devil is depicted as restrained, locked into the bottomless pit and chained. Nevertheless, he still works through intermediaries (as illustrated in Rev. 13, where he acts through the beasts from the sea and the earth). His role can be described as that of a ferocious leashed dog. The securely bound beast can still do damage as far as the length of his chain allows. Outside that range, however, he is definitely limited. The one thing that the devil cannot do is to destroy the church among the nations. God will not let His own be tempted beyond their strength (1 Cor. 10:13).

So what happens when the devil is *loosed* "for a little while" (20:3)? In 20:7-10, he is depicted as the agent for bringing on the end, including his own permanent disposal ("thrown into the lake of fire and brimstone"). The text here (and in its parallels in Rev. 16 and 19) reflects zero damage to the saints in the final battle as they are rescued by the heavenly conqueror (20:9). It seems fitting that the ancient serpent who had caused the exile from the garden of Eden (Gen. 3) would through his final and total defeat be included in the judgment when God would usher in the holy city, New Jerusalem, for the benefit of the saints (21:2).

THE "THOUSAND YEARS"

The thousand year reign, as noted before, is the period between Jesus' first advent and His visible return as Judge. Thus, it coincides with the binding and loosing of Satan (20:2-9). The millennial (1,000 year) reign is referenced only here in all of the Bible, and here in apocalyptic language. Since most of the numbers in Revelation are used symbolically, there is no compulsion to treat the 1,000 years differently. Since 10 is the number of completeness, its compounding simply emphasizes that the return of Christ (the *parousia*) would be a long time after His ascension. St. Augustine and other early church fathers took that view. Although in recent centuries many have promoted the literalizing of the 1,000 years, the main stream of Christian thought has largely "left-behind" that idea as inconsistent with clear teachings throughout Scriptures.[1]

Since the binding and loosing of Satan as well as the 1,000 year reign are placed between the two most explicit final battle scenes in Revelation, they need to be interpreted within that context. Thus, clearly they are eschatological and state a key teaching in relation to the Lord's return as Judge. The 1,000 year reign deals with the lot of those who died in the faith prior to the last day. John does not place this in an earthly setting; he sees it as happening *now* (during the age of the church). The *souls* of the faithful departed continue in a state of *spiritual* blessedness (20:6) as they await the *bodily* resurrection and glorification at the second coming. For John's audience, the "enthronement" and "reign" of the saints is one of immeasurable superiority over that of the oppressive powers that enforced the dictates of the pagan throne during their earthly life. The saints are with Christ, the King of kings and Lord of lords (20:4 and 19:16).

Premillennialists believe that Christ will return visibly for 1,000 years to rule an earthly kingdom before the final judgment.[2] The Bible, however, teaches only one return of Christ after the ascension, and it gives no dating for that. Instead, it urges the church to be watchful and ready at all times. *Postmillennialists* believe in a world evolving toward righteousness, readying it for Christ's return to earth to reign a 1,000 literal years. The wars, terrorism, and scandals of recent centuries have largely debunked that concept.

Thus, those who believe in a symbolic view of the thousand years, namely main stream Christendom, can cling to a view consistent with the clear teachings of Jesus and the Bible. That view gives great comfort and hope for those who die in the faith. It assures them of continual blessedness even up to the time of the Lord's final and singular return. The latter group is often referred to as *amillennialists* because it does not take the thousand years literally. For them, this period is that elastic time frame which stretches out until God's purposes in history are fulfilled.

While the premillennialists have a pessimistic view of history, and the postmillennialists are overly optimistic about man's earthly betterment, amillennialists have the realistic mindset of Jesus' parable of the weeds and the wheat (Matt. 13:24ff.) that good and evil develop together until the separation at the end of the age. Despite their many variations of interpretation, all three views affirm that Jesus will return at the end to unveil God's glorious kingdom for the redeemed and to judge the wicked.

THE ENTHRONEMENT AND REIGN

In John's vision of heaven he sees the souls of the faithful departed sitting on *thrones* in a posture of *judgment*. As they await the Lord's return to raise their bodies "at the last day" (John 6:39ff.), the misfortunes in their earthly lives are left behind. These who were once persecuted and wrongly judged are now able to be "judges" and to declare the frequent refrain of Revelation that God's judgments are "just and true." They affirm that God's punishment of the wicked is duly merited. Similarly, Jesus had assured the disciples who had given up much to follow Him (Matt. 19:28) that in the coming world they would "sit on twelve thrones judging the twelve tribes of Israel." Likewise, Paul declares (1 Cor. 6:2) that the saints will judge the world. In the context of the life of the churches of Asia, it is clear that the enthroned emperor and his cohorts will in time get their judgment for their evil deeds when God's retribution will visit them. The company of the righteous throughout Revelation repeatedly supports these acts of God as just and true in keeping with their considered judgment.

That their *reign* from "thrones" is not a physical one is further supported in 20:6 where it is stated that their thousand year reign is as "*priests* of God and of Christ." Exodus 19:6 had reflected God's plan for His people to be "a kingdom of priests and a holy nation." The concept of the spiritual reign of priests appears also in Rev. 1:6 and 5:9-10 (the new song); it is further reflected in 1 Peter 2:9-10 where the royal priesthood is said to be chosen "to declare the wonderful deeds" of God. As priests while *on earth*, they not only have access to God's presence, but also have the privilege of introducing others to Jesus as they reign with Him who is the King of kings. As the *departed* saints await the second coming, their souls continue in Christ's presence, enthroned and reigning. At the Lord's return, they will do so also with their glorified bodies.

THOSE WHO WILL REIGN

In John's vision he sees the souls of those who were beheaded for their witness to Jesus and God's word. These represent all those who had not denied their Lord by worshipping the beast during their lifetime. Among them are those who had been imprisoned, tested, and had experienced tribulations for the faith. To these Jesus promised "the crown of life" (Rev. 2:10). Similarly, the voice from heaven in Rev. 14:13 had declared of them, "Blessed are the dead who die in the Lord henceforth." By John's time on Patmos, his brother James had been killed by the sword of Herod (Acts 12:2); Paul had already been executed in Rome; and Peter had been crucified there. Antipas, the faithful witness, had been killed at Pergamum (Rev. 2:13). These all, and others, "had not worshiped the beast or its image and had not received its mark." John sees all such faithful witnesses as coming to life and reigning a thousand years (Rev. 20:4).

True believers endured discrimination, persecution, and death in their fidelity to God rather than bowing to the emperor's demand of declaring him "Lord and God," and by refusing to offer the ritual incense at the altar of a pagan priest. For such and for all confessing Christians of the ages, this vision gives comfort. For the benefit of all the saints, John gives them assurance of reigning spiritually with Christ in heaven for the "thousand years" until He returns visibly to earth to raise them to be with Him forever in the New Jerusalem. As Paul wrote, "the sufferings of this present time are not worth comparing with the glory that is to be revealed to us" (Rom. 8:18).

THE REST OF THE DEAD

Those who during their earthly sojourn did not pass "from death to life" in Christ (John 5:24) are described as "the rest of the dead" (Rev. 20:5). They did not embrace the gospel invitation and were unrepentant and unbelieving; they remained dead in their sins, having no hope in God (Eph. 2:1, 12). When their body died, they were confirmed in their separation from God for the "thousand years" until Christ returns as judge. They have no share in the blessedness of the saints, and their future is one of doom. At the final judgment, when they will be resurrected bodily, their destiny is "the lake of fire" (Rev. 20:15). Sadly, they will experience "the second death," hell.

THE FIRST RESURRECTION AND THE SECOND DEATH

Rev. 20:6 presents the fifth of the seven beatitudes found in Revelation. It announces, "Blessed and holy is he who shares in the *first resurrection.* Over such the *second death* has no power...." Since Scripture elsewhere doesn't explicitly mention multiple resurrections, one must search the theology of the Scriptures for clarification. John's Gospel (5:24) sheds light on this passage. There John declares the words of Jesus: "Truly, truly, I say to you, he who hears my word and believes him who sent me, has eternal life; he does not come into judgment, but has passed from death to life." This would suggest that those who live and die in faith while on earth participate in "the first resurrection," a passing from spiritual death to spiritual life. Ephesians 2:4-7 frames this thought similarly like this:

> "God, . . . when we were dead through our trespasses, made us alive together with Christ..., and raised us up with him, and made us sit with him in the heavenly places in Christ Jesus, that in the coming ages he might show the immeasurable riches of his grace...."

Thus, life in Christ begins at the point of entry into faith and never ceases for people who remain faithful unto death. They have died spiritually to sin and have been made spiritually alive when they accepted Jesus as Lord. Even when they eventually die physically, their spirit remains alive in Christ. As Jesus said to Martha, "I am the resurrection and the life; he who believes in me, though he die, yet shall he live, and whoever lives and believes in me, shall never die" (John 11:25-26). Clearly then, he who experiences the first resurrection (entry and continuance in faith) will never die spiritually. Physical death for the one who remains steadfast in the faith becomes the entry point to "the thousand year" reign with Christ. The second death (eternal separation from God) has no power over him.

Sadly, the *second death* (a spiritual one) does have power over the one who remains unbelieving and impenitent; he does <u>not</u> receive the first resurrection when he dies physically because he did not enter Christ's kingdom in his earthly life. Thus, he will not be among those who reign with Christ in the "thousand years" preceding the Lord's return.   Sadly also, he <u>does</u> encounter the second death (eternal separation from God) at his bodily resurrection at the final judgment; his destiny is the lake of fire (Rev. 20:15).

FROM THE MILLENNIUM TO ARMAGEDDON

The millennium closes with the loosing of Satan "for a little while." His activity brings in the end of the age of the church and the return of Christ on the clouds of heaven to raise up all the dead for the final judgment.   There the saints will be ushered into a glorious eternity with the Father and the Lamb.   At the same time the wicked will be "thrown into the lake of fire."

The thousand year binding and restraint of Satan, as described in Rev. 20:1-6, is an interlude between two depictions of the gathering of the armies of the earth against the saints of God.   In both cases, the scenes end with the total destruction of Satan's forces by the heavenly conqueror with no losses on God's side.   In each case the battle is quickly terminated.

Rev. 20:7-10 uses new imagery (that of "Gog and Magog") to describe the same battle that is depicted in Rev. 16:12-21, there referred to as Armageddon, and in Rev. 19:11-21 at the conquest by the divine rider of the white horse.   While there are other scenes in Revelation that show God's judgment on a perverse world, these three battle accounts merit special consideration because of their striking similarities in describing the final attack of the combined antiChristian forces against the church and her Lord.   Each of the three accounts shows an escalation in the intensity of opposition by secular forces against the church.   While no age is without troubling trials and tribulations, it is clear that the devil marshals a desperate final attack as the end draws near and God draws down the curtain of history.

While the Gog and Magog battle scene of Rev. 20:7-10 is a recycling of the singular victory at Armageddon and by the heavenly armies in Rev. 19:11-21, yet the popular picture of these three depictions is often thought of under the term "Armageddon."   In each of the three accounts, God's people are "more than conquerors through him who loved us" (Rom. 8:37). It will be instructive to examine the unique details, as well as the similarities of these three battle portrayals as their message unfolds.

ARMAGEDDON BRINGS ON THE END

The sixth and seventh bowls of God's wrath tell the story of Armageddon (Rev.16:12-21). Three foul spirits like frogs go forth from the unholy three of the dragon, the beast, and the false prophet. They gather the kings of the whole world for the final battle at Armageddon on "the great day of God." The site is a famous Old Testament battle ground. The day comes unannounced (like a thief), and God's victory is complete: "It is done!" It comes through decisive "acts of God" (including lightning, thunder, and a great earthquake). The great city Babylon and the cities of the nations are devastated. Every mountain and island disappears. The surviving men curse God for the fury of the immense hail stones.

Unique to this final battle account is the movement from the Euphrates site of ancient Babylon to the symbolic Babylon, Rome. The former Babylon was destroyed by means of an invasion by the Persian king Cyrus, using the path of the dried up river bed. The latter Babylon's destruction is further reflected and lamented in Rev. 17 and 18 which follow immediately. Other unique points include the unclean frogs (a fitting mouth piece for the demons); the surprise of the "coming" (like a thief); the beatitude celebrating those who are prepared (awake and clothed); and the destruction brought on by the forces of nature, reminiscent of the earlier battles at Megiddo in the time of Deborah, and later of King Josiah. Perhaps surprisingly, there are men left alive to curse God. The apocalyptic retelling of the final battle in chapters 19 and 20 adds intensity, and takes care of that detail!

HEAVEN'S CAVALRY RIDES ON TO VICTORY

Rev. 19:11-21 presents a unique parallel to the Armageddon battle. The scene follows immediately on the account of the marriage supper of the Lamb. A new meal, described as "the great supper of God" (19:17), is a veritable fowl feast. To get to that point, John sees heaven opened and a white horse, an appropriate symbol. (Roman generals traditionally rode a white horse when celebrating a military "triumph".) The rider is followed by the armies of heaven, clad in fine linen (the vesture of the saints), riding on horses of the same hue (white, the symbol of victory). They ride forth against their earthly opponents.

The identity of the lead horseman presents unmistakable Christology. His name is one of mystery (19:12, perhaps an allusion to the divine name in Exodus 3:14). He is called: *"Faithful and True"* (an accolade regularly offered God throughout Revelation by heaven's heirs); *"the Word of God"* (through whom God has spoken; Heb. 1:1-2 and John 1:1, 14); and *"the King of kings and the Lord of lords"* (indicating Jesus' headship over all earthly potentates, including pagan emperors!). His penetrating vision reflects back on Rev. 1:14; He sees and knows all. His many diadems indicate his rule over many kingdoms. The robe dipped in blood reflects His prior redemptive work (5:9 and 7:14) and foreshadows His future role as judge when he would tread "the winepress of the fury of the wrath of God" (19:13, 15; see also 14:19-20). The sharp sword that issues from His mouth is the word of God which both reveals the love of God and serves as the only weapon He needs as judge. (See also 1:16 and Heb. 4:12.) He will rule over the opponent nations with total authority ("a rod of iron"; see also 12:5 and Psalm 2:9).

In another vision John sees the aftermath of the final battle without describing an actual combat. When God takes on the enemy, there is no contest. He rules! In the portrayal of the fowl feast, John adapts the vision of Ezekiel (#39:7-20) where God summons the vultures to assemble and to feast on the slain warriors of Gog of Magog. In

John's vision the slain opponents are the idolaters of the nations. Their armies were slain by a sword that issues from the mouth of the heavenly horseman (the word of God). The same rider (Jesus) earlier had ridden triumphantly into Jerusalem to conquer through the cross and the empty tomb, as recorded in the four Gospels.

The beast and the false prophet had led the opposition against those who are steadfast in their worship of God. The fate of the evil ones is to be thrown alive into the lake of fire. This will happen at the same time that Satan, the dragon, joins them there; his story is told in the next chapter (Rev. 20).

This vision, like that of Armageddon in Rev. 16, is not a literal description of the end. It is symbolism at its best. Though the apocalyptic imagery may seem repulsive, its message is real. At the end of time, the conflict between the forces of good and evil will be over. The outcome of the final showdown in the spiritual struggle of life is the decisive victory of Christ for His followers and the resultant defeat of the forces of evil, led by Satan and his proponents. The victory is won by the word of Christ alone, without any military help from His followers. They will be "along for the ride" and the victory celebration (19:9, 14).

Unique details in this telling of the final showdown include the high Christology presented (compared to that of the Armageddon scene); the victory ride of the heavenly King and His armies; their attire of fine linen, appropriate for the bride of Christ (19:9, 14); absence of reference to any earthly site; focus on the saving work of Jesus (as compared to the Armageddon focus on the power of the almighty God); the fowl feasting on the slain warriors (there are no human "left-overs" to curse, as in the vision of the last two "bowls"); and the final disposal of the beast and false prophet into the lake of fire.

THE RESCUE FROM GOG AND MAGOG

At the end of the millennium, Satan is described as loosed from his chain in the bottomless pit. Then, "for a little while," he will be allowed to attack the church *directly* with his campaign of deceit as he stirs up the nations. "Gog and Magog" are named here in apposition to "the nations." While in the vision of Ezekiel 38-39 Gog of Magog attacks the land of Israel and is destroyed by divine intervention, John here expands the threat and the divine rescue to cosmic proportions (the four corners of the earth). To identify and single out particular nations, as some have done, is misguided; "their number is like the sand of the sea" (20:8).

In Jewish literature Gog and Magog are analogous to the enemies of God's people. As at Armageddon, Satan's forces are gathered and poised for battle, here at "the beloved city." Again, when the situation seems desperate, there is an intervention from heaven. The beloved city is wherever God's people are gathered. Historically, they had gathered around the tabernacle in their wilderness years; later, at the temple in "the holy city." Ultimately, their goal is "New Jerusalem." Wherever God's people are gathered, He promises to be in their midst (Matt. 18:20) to shield and to preserve.

Fire came down from heaven to consume the apostate nations that were in the attack mode at "the beloved city." For the deceiving devil there are appropriate "accommodations." He is spared, fittingly, for a new confinement and punishment. Where else, but in the lake of fire (hell)? There he joins his henchmen, the beast and the false prophet, forever.

Unique to the third version of the Armageddon account, the Gog and Magog scene has a greater air of finality. Here Satan is finally and completely put down. The reference to the beloved city symbolizes the church universal, rescued by divine intervention (the redemptive work of Jesus). Also, there is a tie to the millennium, which has immediately preceded the end here described. Hereafter, Revelation lists no further battles and no further tribulations for the saints. The judgment and the joys of New Jerusalem bring the story into the glorious and everlasting future for God's faithful folk.

COMMON POINTS IN THE THREE SCENES

The depiction of the three scenes of the final battle repeats similar themes. Through apocalyptic imagery they assure the believing and confessing church that the struggle of the life of faith is worth it. The future glory of the redeemed more than compensates for the sufferings of the present age. Already those who have died in faith are enjoying the presence of the Lord as their souls live and reign with him. Those who still remain alive have the further assurance that God will finally come to restore the body with the soul in the glorious resurrection that immediately follows the final defeat of the oppressive forces of Satan's kingdom. The story of that final battle and victory is stated three times to emphasize its certainty and to lift the spirits of God's own. That victory will come "in the twinkling of an eye" (1 Cor. 15:51-52). It will be everywhere at once, not only at Megiddo, or Babylon, or Jerusalem; and it will be at a time when God's purposes in history are complete, a time known only to God. Despite the novel ways of telling the same story, there are many common notes and themes in these three accounts (in chapters 16, 19, and 20). They include the following:

Common Points	Rev.16:12-21	Rev.19:11-21	Rev.20:7-10
1. The unholy three are active	v. 13	vv. 19-20	vv. 7-10
2. They deceive	v. 14	v. 20	v. 8
3. They use the kings	vv. 12, 14	vv. 18-19	v. 8
4. The whole world is involved	v. 14	vv. 18-19, 21	vv. 8-9
5. The foes are gathered	vv. 14, 16	vv. 17-19	v. 8
6. There is a great battle	v. 14	vv. 19-21	vv. 8-9
7. The great day	v. 14	v. 17	v. 7
8. God's fury is revealed	v. 19	vv. 15, 20-21	vv. 9-10
9. Retribution from heaven	vv. 18-21	vv. 14-15	vv. 9-10
10. The victory is instant	v. 17	vv. 20-21	v. 9
11. There is finality	vv. 19-21	vv. 20-21	vv. 9-10
12. The lake of fire	-------	v. 20	v. 10

AT THE GREAT WHITE THRONE

The Apostles' Creed states the belief that "He will come again to judge the quick and the dead." The culmination of the hope for blessedness is found in the event at the great white throne. The scene in Rev. 20:11-15 includes these notable points:

1. The judgment throne is unique and superior.
2. Planet earth as now known disappears.
3. The two types of books are critical.
4. All will appear; none are overlooked at the judgment.
5. All of God's foes are thrown into the lake of fire.

1. THE THRONE IS GREAT AND WHITE.

Great, because it is the throne of God, who together with the Lamb is the supreme ruler and judge of the universe. Before that throne all must stand, including those who occupied earthly thrones, such as Emperors Nero and Domitian, whose evils are very much in mind in the background of the Apocalypse. It is a *white* throne, symbolic of the purity and correctness of the divine judgments. Throughout the Apocalypse God's actions are declared as just and true. Before this throne every one will get a fair review. None will be able to claim collusion or partiality. At this throne saints and angels will consent to God's judgments as "just and true."

2. THE EARTH DISAPPEARS.

"From his presence earth and sky fled away" (20:11). Jesus had said, "Heaven and earth will pass away" (Mark 13:31). That statement is echoed in greater detail in 2 Peter 3:10, "The heavens will pass away with a loud noise . . . and the earth . . . will be burned up." It seems duly fitting that this earth, polluted and perverted by the sins of humanity be cleared away for God to replace it with "a new heaven and a new earth" (21:1) for the enjoyment of His beloved followers.

3. THE BOOKS "WERE OPENED" (20:12).

Each individual's words and works, by their very enactment, become entries in the book of the divine recorder of deeds. People are judged at the great white throne on the basis of their merit. The sad fact is, as Paul states, "No one is righteous, no, not one" (Rom.3:10). The Psalmist responds to this dilemma, "If thou, O Lord, shouldst mark iniquities, Lord, who shall stand? But there is forgiveness with thee. . ."(Ps.130:3). And so, there is another book, the book of life. It is posited on the good news that "the blood of Jesus his Son cleanses us from all sin" (1 John 1:17). Those who cling to the ransom paid by Jesus have their names recorded in this book. They do not come under judgment. They are saved by grace. John found the symbolism of the book of life very meaningful, referring to it repeatedly (3:5; 13:8; 17:8; 20:12, 15; and 21:27).

4. ALL APPEAR.

The great and small (v. 12) stand as equals before the judgment throne. Kings and paupers alike appear in resurrected bodies to receive their just due. There is no way of escaping the presence of God (Ps. 139:7-12). No one is overlooked. No matter where, when, or how one dies and is buried enables absenteeism at the great white throne. Even the sea and Death and Hades surrender their dead. All will meet the Judge. For those enrolled in the book of life, it will be a deliverance far more excellent than any of the judges (deliverers) up to Samuel's time could provide. For the others, their own book of deeds will render the verdict.

5. THE LAKE OF FIRE IS HELL.

It is the repository of the demonic forces (the beast, the false prophet, and the devil) and their retinue, all those who bear the mark of the beast. Finally, Death and Hades are thrown in with them. This is the second death, the eternal separation of body and soul from God for those who in their lives were spiritually dead to Him. By way of contrast, those recorded in the book of life will enjoy the eternal blessedness of the presence of the Father and the Lamb in the glorious New Jerusalem. For their benefit, Revelation closes with the magnificent vision of heaven, and with the prayer of the church that their Lord come quickly.

---

[1]For a consistent and definitive study of the Biblical texts on the millennium, see The End Times: A Study on Eschatology and Millennialism. A Report of the Commission of Theology and Church Relations of the Lutheran Church Missouri Synod, September, 1989.

[2]Hal Lindsey in his Late Great Planet Earth (Grand Rapids, Zondervan, 1970) has championed this view. Tim LaHaye and Jerry Jenkins through their "Left Behind" series of novels have built on these sensationalized views of Lindsey.

CHAPTER VIII

BABYLON AND NEW JERUSALEM

BIBLE READINGS

1. **Babylon**.
   a. <u>Primary</u>: Rev. 14:8; 16:19; 17:1-19:5.
   b. <u>Corollary</u>: Gen. 11:1-9; 12:1; 2 Kings 24-25:21; Psalm 137; Jer. 51-52; Daniel 3-6; 1 Peter 5:13.
2. **New Jerusalem**.
   a. <u>Primary</u>: Rev. 21:1-22:5.
   b. <u>Corollary</u>: Ezek. 47:1-12; Matt. 4:5; 27:53; Gal. 4:21-31; Rev. 14:1-5; 20:9 (and 16:16).

CLASHING SYMBOLS

As the reader moves to the climax of Revelation, he discovers that the story becomes a "tale of two cities." After "sin city" is identified and her demise is depicted and lamented, the "holy city" comes clearly into view. It is the long awaited "promised land." The journey to this heavenly city had been beset with serious and severe sufferings and stumbling blocks. However, as the New Jerusalem comes down and into view, the perseverance of the saints is most amply rewarded. Let us, then, look at the opposing portraits of these two cities. Later, we shall offer some thought provoking questions to guide our discussion of the message of these "clashing symbols." We begin with Babylon, or "sin city."

BABYLON

Babylon from earliest times was associated with the sins of pride, presumption, and power-mongering. Her long history is marked with continual examples. Already at the "Tower of Babel" (Gen. 11:1-9), she set herself up so as to presume on God by building a tower that would reach into the heavens and make a name for herself. "Babel" means "gate to God," and is generally seen as a denial of God's way to heaven. God's way would be through the blood of His own Son, a ransom paid for the wages of sin (death). God's way was/is acceptance of the way of grace, achieved through Jesus' substitution for man's inability to remain obedient to God's will and plan. Babel's way was to make a "gate-way to God" through her own effort. It amounted to a "declaration of independence," a denial of God's way of grace, and an assertion of man's equality with God. It is reminiscent of the original sin in Eden, wanting "to be like God, knowing good and evil." It is a circumvention of the mystery of God's love and forgiveness. Later stages of Babylon's history would repeat that spirit of independence and arrogance all the way to the time of Saint John and beyond.

Babylon's infamy resurfaced with devastating effect on an international scale at the time of Prophet Jeremiah. The abomination committed in the sack and destruction of Jerusalem and her temple (God's house!) is the unparalleled low-point in Old Testament history. When the "holy city" of the "children of Israel" was destroyed, so were the "holy place" and "the holy of holies" of the temple where God was seen to dwell.

Later, during the long captivity in Babylon, Nebuchadnezzar would add insult to injury as he fostered the erection of a 90-foot tall image which Jews and others were to worship, or be persecuted for non-compliance. The book of <u>Daniel</u> tells the story of the persecution of Daniel's friends all the way to the fiery furnace; only after the miraculous deliverance of Daniel's three friends, is the king ready to acknowledge "the Most High God." In a later story, Daniel himself is thrown into the lion's den for his refusal to worship a subsequent Babylonian king. Ultimately this Babylon, whose hanging gardens had become one of the Seven Wonders of the Ancient World, would herself fall.

In Jeremiah 51, the prophet is quite explicit about God's judgment on Babylon, which had been such a scourge on His people. She would be utterly destroyed and become a horror among the nations (Jer. 51:41-44). Babylon's demise was described as a just recompense for her foul deeds (vv. 54-56). The inevitability of her judgment is symbolized by Jeremiah's writing "in a book all the evil that should come upon Babylon"(v. 60), and sinking that book with a stone in the

Euphrates. To protect themselves, God's people were warned to flee Babylon (v. 45).

In the apostolic age Rome took on the identity of a "new" Babylon because of the scourge she had become for the city, temple, and people of Jerusalem (now scattered abroad). The long siege and cruel carnage and devastation leading up to Jerusalem's fall in 70 A.D. are well documented in Josephus' historical works. The arch of Titus in Rome perpetuates the woeful memories. Not surprisingly, then, 1 Peter 5:13 refers to Rome as Babylon. Near the end of Revelation, John refers to Babylon <u>six</u> times (14:8; 16:19; 17:5; and in 18:2, 10, and 21). Interestingly, this matches the number of times the word "woe" (ουαι) and the phrase "no more" are used in the "lament chapter" (#18). Babylon's judgment would be commensurate with the severity of her persecutions.

John has much to say about Babylon in Revelation. He states that she:
- is a harlot and a beast (17:1-5);
- has drunk the blood of the saints (17:6);
- is on seven hills [commonly associated with Rome] (17:9);
- is powerful [like Babylon was in antiquity; her beast has ten horns], (17:3);
- is a gathering of many conquered nations, as was Old Babylon (17:15);
- will destroy herself through internal strife (17:16-17);
- is fallen (18:2);
- is mourned by:
  - monarchs [rulers, people of power and influence], (18:9f.);
  - merchants [traders, people of commerce and wealth], (18:11ff.); and, by
  - mariners ["middle-men," sea-farers who can "deliver the goods"], (18:17ff.);
- is to be fled by God's people [18:4];
- will be utterly destroyed, symbolized by a great stone thrown into the sea (18:21-23);
- is totally deserving of her judgments, which are "just and true" (19:2).

The lament over Babylon is highly reminiscent of the "lamentations" over Jerusalem, which was destroyed by the ancient Babylonians, at the time of Jeremiah. This extends even to the literary form of the lament. Lamentations has a 6-fold acrostic which bemoans Jerusalem's fate (despite the fact that the book has 7 multiples of 22 verses—22 being the number of letters in the Hebrew alphabet). Six is the number of sin and evil, and thus also utterly befitting lamentation over sin and evil. Similarly, John formally structures 6 **"no more"** statements in Rev. 18:21-23, repeating the Greek formula, ου μη ...ετι in each of the 6 "no more" laments. The six laments include 3 sights and 3 sounds. Three sights will "no more" be seen: Babylon herself; her craftsmen; and her lights. In alternate verses there is also reference to 3 sounds "no more" to be heard: the sound of music, of the millstone, and of the voice of the bride and groom.

Such utter devastation, nevertheless, is seen as meriting a four-fold "Hallelujah!" Nowhere else, in the New Testament is this word used. Truly, the undoing of all evil is an answer to the Christian's fervent prayer, "Deliver us from evil; for thine is the kingdom and the power and the glory forever. Amen!"

NEW JERUSALEM

When selecting a place to live and work, people pay dearly for what realtors and other recruiters trumpet as "location, location, location." I have lived in a city whose Chamber of Commerce billed her as "the best location in the nation." I have visited both the Dead Sea and Death Valley. There is little doubt as to where I'd rather live. New Jerusalem and Babylon are the contrasting places vying for influence over the lives of people in Revelation. One is the place of life; the other of death.

Before comparing Babylon and Jerusalem, however, one should note that there are also two Jerusalem's that require definition. Galatians 4:21-31 does it well by contrasting them as follows through the allegory of the two covenants.

113

The "present" Jerusalem	The coming Jerusalem
-is born of a slave mother (v. 24-25)	-is born free (v. 26)
-according to the flesh (v. 23)	-according to promise (v. 23)
-Mt. Sinai in Arabia (v. 24)	-the Jerusalem above (v. 26)
-Ishmael, born of Hagar (v. 29)	-Isaac, born of Sarah (v. 28)
-will not inherit (v. 30)	-will inherit (v. 30)
-persecutor (v. 29)	-persecuted (v. 29)
-Judaizers (v. 31)	-Christians (v. 31)
(in Revelation: Babylon)	(in Revelation: New Jerusalem)

Jerusalem is called the "holy" city, properly so because of the presence there of God's temple and many of Jesus' works of salvation. There is utter irony, then, that she should become a city "where their Lord was crucified" (11:8), and allegorically be called "Sodom and Egypt" (11:8), and eventually be superseded as prime persecutor by "Babylon," the city of 7 hills (17:9), and "the mother of harlots" (17:5).

However, whenever Jerusalem is mentioned by name in Revelation, it is always in reference to the holy city or New Jerusalem. We shall proceed, then, with the positive identity for the "Jerusalem above," since the former Jerusalem has been left in the shadows by John [except for a few oblique references such as the allegorical reference in 11:8; and to the Mt. Zion or the "beloved city" as the place of the redeemed or of the punishment of the evil ones], Rev. 14:1-5 and 20:9.

Everything about "Jerusalem" is positive for God's people. Babylon's story had been totally negative. In a positive vein, there are some "negatives" about "Jerusalem." For New Jerusalem there are seven things that are described as "no more" (οὐκ...ετι). Using the οὐκ...ετι formula, John declares that New Jerusalem has "no more": 1) sea, 21:1; 2) death, 21:4; 3) mourning, 21:4; 4) crying, 21:4; 5) pain, 21:4; 6) anything accursed, 22:3; 7) night, 22:5.

Unlike the 6 "no mores" of Babylon in 18:21-23 (the number of evil and lamentation), Jerusalem's 7 "no mores" reflect fullness— fullness of joy as Rev. 21 states that there is "**no more**"

1) sea, such as separated the exiled John from the beloved on the mainland;
2) death, the lot of martyrs like Antipas (2:13), and of mankind generally;
3) mourning, the feelings that come with bereavement;
4) crying, the expression of grief or pain;
5) pain, the experience of suffering (be that mental, physical, or spiritual);
6) anything accursed, that which is compromised because of sin;
7) night, the time of ignorance and wickedness.

Besides these 7 things, John relates [without use of the ουκ...ετι formula]   that other things are not there either because of the appearance of the One Who makes all things new. Thus:

- New Jerusalem needs no temple (21:22) because God and the Lamb are there;
- the sun and moon become obsolete (21:23) because of the radiance of God and the Lamb [Who is the Light of the World], (John 8:12; 9:5); and,
- all people who are evil to the core are excluded (21:8).

The "positives" about New Jerusalem are as remarkable as they are numerous. John declares regarding New Jerusalem that:
1) she originates in heaven, the source of all good (21:2);
2) the anticipation is intense, as that of a bride prepared for her husband (21:2);
3) God and his people dwell together (21:3);
4) everything is new, trustworthy, and true (21:5);
5) the water of life is given freely (21:6);
6) the redeemed are claimed in God's family (21:7);
7) the church is the Bride of the Lamb (Christ) (21:9);
8) she is radiant and precious beyond words (21:11, 18-21);
9) she includes all the faithful of both old and new covenants, as reflected by the repeated use of 12 (the number of the faithful);
10) the 12 tribes represent the former times; the 12 apostles the latter days;

11) all those who are in the Lamb's "book of life" are there (21:27);
12) it is measured [for preservation], 21:15 (see 11:1-2 and Zech. 2:1-5);
13) the cube shape promises the presence of the Holy One [as in the cubed "holy of holies" of the temple], 21:16;
14) its wall symbolizes security (21:17);
15) the numbers 12,000 [all the faithful], and 144 [the faithful of both covenants,12x12] reflect on inclusion of all God's people (21:16-17);
16) the gates remain open because there are no enemies anymore (21:25);
17) those who practice the evil so typical of Babylon are excluded (21:8, 27);
18) the water of life flows perpetually (22:1-2);
19) no good thing will be withheld, not even the fruits of the tree of life (22:2);
20) the tree of life gives healing for the nations (22:2); and,
21) the saints will reign forever with God (22:5).

In conclusion, as we compare and contrast New Jerusalem with Babylon, we do well to examine Krodel's tabular listing (pages 352-354). He lists 17 points of comparison (5 in the introduction of the cities; 7 in the vision itself; and, 5 more in the conclusion). Two cities could hardly be more opposite in present focus and future reward than Babylon and New Jerusalem. While the one is the paradigm of idolatry and exploitation, the other is the model of fidelity and grace. Those who aspire to New Jerusalem anchor their hopes in the glorious future which abides forever, indeed long after the earth-bound Babylon has passed away in infamy (Heb. 13:14).

FOR STUDY AND REFLECTION ON:

BABYLON

1. How do the Tower of Babel, the Babylonian Empire that captured Jerusalem and exiled her best people, and kings like Nebuchadnezzar relate to how the "New Babylon" (Rome) affected the worship and life of God's people?

2. Who is the "she at Babylon" mentioned in 1 Peter 5:13? Why
   does the apostle use this description?

3. How is this "she" different from the "she" of Rev. 17:5, 6, and
   18?

4. Is the "beast" of 17:3-5 related to the beast of 13:1? If so,
   how?

5. Whom had the "harlot of Babylon" seduced? (Rev. 17-18)

6. How does the harlot of Babylon's dress and behavior (Rev.
   17:2-6) relate to:
   a.   modern advertising?
   b.   the products of the entertainment industry (e.g.,
        movies, TV talk shows, "soaps," and internet
        offerings that are sexually provocative, violent, or
        self-serving?
   c.   The "modern" attitude that behavior is acceptable "as
        long as you feel good" about it?

7. With the help of a commentary (e.g., those of Becker, Brighton,
   Krodel, Morris, Mounce, or Murphy), answer these questions:
   a.   Who are "the dwellers on earth" ? (17:8)   Note:
        knowing this makes a big difference on how you see
        the book's message.
   b.   How does Rev. 17:9 locate Babylon for John's
        people?
   c.   Does the king "who is" (the one between #5 and #7,
        namely, #6) have a relationship to the #666 of Rev.
        13:18?   Explain.
   d.   Note: Rev. 13:18 and 17:19 both "call for wisdom."
        Is that a coincidence? Or, is there a message here
        (especially since these are the only places in Rev. that
        this occurs)?

8. Horns (17:12) are symbols of power. The number 10 often
   indicates totality.
   a.   Do you "take" this #10 in Rev. 17:12-14
        symbolically? literally?

b. Explain what bearing this has in regard to the existence of "power-mongers" who may oppose God's ways.

9. Is there a relation in 17:16-18 to the eventual self-destruction of the harlot/beast/city and the fulfillment of God's purposes? If so, what bearing has this on the faith of God's people?

10. Note the command of 18:4 to forsake Babylon. Correlate this with a similar earlier command regarding Babylon (see Jeremiah 51:45). Why should God's people flee "sin city"?

11. Mourners of Babylon.
   a. What have all three groups in common ?   (monarchs [17:9], merchants [17:11], and, mariners [17:17])
   b. Do any of them try to save their "beloved" city?
   c. What does that say of the loyalties of "the masses" who tolerate, defend, and/or enjoy "sin-city"?

12. Note the repeated elements of the dirges of the 3 lamenting groups listed (in #11a, above). What point(s) do the repeated refrains emphasize?

13. How does Psalm 137 relate to the lives of the people of God:
   a. during the Babylonian exile in the O.T.?
   b. during John's exile on the isle of Patmos?
   c. during the lives of contemporary "saints" who experience life's "tribulations," or persecutions, for the faith [as they anticipate future deliverance from their own personal "exile"]?

14. Note: Rev. 19:1-6 has the only "hallelujah's" of the New Testament. Are Christians allowed to rejoice when those who tolerate and support evil at the expense of Christians get their "true and just" (19:2) "desserts"?

NEW JERUSALEM

1. How do each of the 7 things that are "no more" (sea, death, mourning, crying, pain, anything accursed, night), when John's people arrive at New Jerusalem, reflect an improvement over their earthly life (see Rev.21:1, 4; 22:3, 5)?

2. How is New Jerusalem different from the "Old" Jerusalem?
    a. In Rev. 21:1-4?
    b. In 21:10-21?
    c. In 21:22-27?
    d. In 22:1-5?

3. Compare the picture of New Jerusalem in 22:1-5 with Ezekiel 47:1-12.
    a. How are they similar?
    b. How different (e.g., in respect to the temple and the water)?
    c. What do these two pictures tell you about heaven?

4. What are the two things that New Jerusalem symbolizes? (See Rev. 21:2, 9-10.)

5. Coming down.
    a. List whatever spiritually uplifting thoughts you have regarding New Jerusalem's "coming down" from heaven (see Rev. 21:2, 10-12).
    b. What relation is there between that and the "coming down" of Jesus?
    c. Does that reassure you?

6. What "good news" do you get from the fact that New Jerusalem:
    a. is "cube-shaped" (21:16)? [Note: The holy of holies was cubed also.]
    b. has measurements of "12" stadia and "144" cubits (21:16-17)?

c. has 12 gates and foundations (21:12-14)?

7. What "good news" do you find in the promise of:
   a. the water of life (22:1; see also John 4:7-15)?
   b. the New Jerusalem being enclosed by walls (21:12-15)?
   c. the "stones" of the city (21:18-21)?
   d. the city's lights (21:23-24)?
   e. the open gates (21:25-27)?
   f. the river of life (22:1)?
   g. the tree of life (22:2)?

8. Comment on the temple after consulting Rev. 21:22 and John 2:16-22.
   a. What (or Who?) is the temple's true identity?(You may also wish to refer to 1 Cor. 3:16-17, and 6:19; and, 2 Cor. 6:16; Eph. 2:21; and, Rev. 3:12; 7:15; and 11:1, 2, 19.)
   b. What is the purpose of the temple (in the Bible)? Still today?
   c. How does Rev. 21:22 provide a necessary corrective to the thinking of those who say that the temple must be rebuilt in Jerusalem before Jesus returns?

9. What is the role of the Lamb:
   a. for the saints in heaven (see 21:22-22:5)?
   b. for the "saints" who are still on earth? (You may wish to consult a concordance to discover the Lamb's role in Rev. 5-19.)

10.   Names.
   a. Whose names are found on:
        i. the gates of the city (21:12)?
        ii. the foundations (21:14)?
   b. What message does that impart?

11. Comment on the Lord's word in Exodus 33:20, "You cannot see my face...and live," in the light of Rev. 22:4-5. (You may perhaps also reflect on the contribution of Genesis 32:26-30.)

12. Write a few sentences on what you expect or hope heaven to be like. Be prepared to share it.

CHAPTER IX

THE BRIDE AND THE HARLOT

1. **The Bride**
   a. Primary: Rev. 12:1-6; 13-17; 19:6-9; 21:2-14; 22:17.
   b. Corollary: Isaiah 25:6-8; 54:1-7; 61:10; 62:5; Jeremiah 2:2-3; Ezek.16:7-8; Hosea 3; Matt. 9:14-15; 22:1-14; 25:1-13; John 3:29; Eph. 5:23-32; and, 2 Cor. 11:2.

2. **The Harlot**
   a. Primary: Rev. 17:1-18.
   b. Corollary: Jer. 51; Ezek. 16 and 23; Nahum 3; Rev. 18:1-19:5; 19:17-21; 21:7-8.

CLASHING SYMBOLS

Closely allied with Revelation's "tale of two cities" (Babylon and New Jerusalem) is the struggle between the harlot and the bride. These very opposite symbols are also introduced and developed in the latter half of the book.

The bride is introduced first under the figure of the woman who gives birth to the unique child of promise (12:1-6). Next, she is depicted as being nourished in the wilderness for 1260 days, alternately stated as "for a time, and times, and a half a time" (12:6, 14). She is identical with the 144,000 redeemed who celebrate on Mt. Zion "who have not defiled themselves with women, for they are chaste [virgins], . . . and in their mouth no lie was found. . . " (14:4-5). The "bride" picture comes to full bloom, finally, in 19:6-9 and in 21:1-11, where the bride is clearly depicted as "wife of the Lamb."

The bride's antagonist is first designated as "the harlot" in 17:1, and her decadence and demise are described lengthily from 17:1 to 19:5. Her identity as "Babylon" is first noted in 14:8, and her fate is mentioned finally in 21:8 as "the second death" in the "lake that burns with fire and sulphur."

THE BRIDE

The woman, who appears as a sign surrounded by the sun, moon, and stars (12:1), eventually is identified as the Bride. The sun, that clothes her with light, signals her radiance; the moon beneath her feet speaks of her dominion; and, the 12 stars in her crown depict her royalty. She is the clear antithesis of the scarlet harlot of Rev. 17.

This pregnant woman of John's vision is the "true Israel" in her Messianic expectation. The child she carried had been promised from the beginning of man's need for a Savior, first to Eve, the mother of the living. Successively, the promise was renewed through patriarchs, kings, and prophets. Mary became the vehicle of fulfillment to the community of faith, the ideal Israel. At the start of chapter 12, Israel is the community through which the child came; in the last section of chapter 12, the woman has advanced in time to represent the church in her time of persecution. In keeping with apocalyptic style, the two eras fuse into a single community of faith; and, the woman represents all of it, the community of saints of both O.T. and N.T. times.

The great red dragon clearly identifies with the scarlet woman of chapter 17 who sits on the scarlet beast, committing her murderous seductions. The dragon's heads, horns, and diadems reflect his great cunning, power, and dominion. His casting down of a third of the stars of heaven (12:4) link him with the havoc wreaked on the third of the stars by the fourth trumpet (8:12). His intent to devour the new-born child calls to mind the plan of King Herod the Great to slay the child of Mary (Matt. 2).

However, the woman's child withstood all threats, overcoming the threat of kings (including later also Herod Antipas), of Satan, and of opposing religious leaders as He glorified the Father through His triumphant resurrection and ascension. The woman's child in time would shepherd His people with his strong and protective "rod of iron." Not only were Satan's plots of destroying Him at His birth thwarted; also, Jesus' unique death on the cross would be the prelude to His resurrection triumph over the grave for all those who would come under His shepherding rule. As He visibly left His people, He ascended triumphantly to the throne above all thrones. There He sits at the Father's right hand.

The woman, having been blessed with the child, however, still awaits her final deliverance. While she, who is God's faithful people, waits for the Lord's glorious return, she is nourished. The place of nourishment is the wilderness. Holy Scripture often describes the wilderness as the place for sustaining God's people until better days would dawn. The nation Israel had been established there during the Exodus. Elijah twice was sustained in wilderness settings as he fled from Ahab or Jezebel. Joseph and Mary fled with the infant Jesus through the wilderness to Egypt to avoid the murderous Herod. The wilderness was where God had nourished Israel as He fed and led them to a better land.

The wilderness represents a complete spiritual detachment from the world (from the great city, Babylon). It is a necessary preparation for the glorious future of New Jerusalem. As the dragon proceeds to make warfare against the woman's offspring (12:17), the Christians, they are sustained. The same God Who had carried their forebears "as on eagles' wings" to Sinai and had delivered them through "the miracle of the sea" (Exod. 14-15) now shields them.

The purpose of the vision is to assure God's people that even when they are under persecution or the threat of martyrdom, He has provided them a spiritual refuge so that they can withstand the devil. The time of this divine refuge corresponds exactly with the period of persecution. As long as they require refuge, God will provide it.

The woman's story resumes in chapter 19. There her marriage is imminent. Her perseverance is rewarded! The woman who has faithfully endured her wilderness life becomes the wife of the Lamb. Rev. 19:6-9 exults with a mighty "Hallelujah" over the reign of the Almighty Lord. The long-awaited consummation of the hope of the faithful has come. The period of betrothal and of expectant waiting is ending. The fullness of joy arrives amid intimacy with the Good Shepherd Who willed to become the Lamb of God.

"Let us rejoice and be glad!" Thus sings the heavenly throng regarding the Lamb's marriage to the Bride. The only other time the N. T. uses these two verbs together is in Matt. 5:12 where the rejoicing is over the great heavenly reward for those who were reviled and persecuted for Jesus' sake. Clearly, John echoes the same thought regarding the reward of fidelity. Not only is the payoff a great one; it also endures forever!

The marriage with Christ is described both as a gift and as an active response by the faithful bride. "It was granted her," John says, "to be clothed with fine linen, bright and pure." Her clothes has been made white through being washed in the blood of the Lamb. Redemption is the gift of God which the bride wears as wedding gown. This dress is in sharp contrast to the gaudy clothes of the drunken whore of Babylon (17:4-6). The latter is dressed in purple and scarlet, the colors of Rome's imperial majesty and decadence. The bride's white dress symbolizes purity (in contrast to the fornication of the harlot). White is the symbol of purity and of victory for those who are headed for heaven. Thus, the Laodiceans were urged to get "white garments" to cover their shame (3:18); the martyrs receive white robes as they wait out God's timetable (6:11); the numberless multitude before the throne rejoices in white robes (7:9, 13); and, the armies of heaven follow the triumphant King of kings on His white horse, wearing "fine linen, white and pure," while also riding white horses (19:11-16). The harlot, on the other hand, is a "material girl" displaying gold and precious stones (17:4); but, the bride's only adornment is her bright and pure linen that represents "the righteous deeds of the saints" (19:8).

While the union with the Lamb is a gift of God's grace, it also involves active preparation by the bride. She "has made herself ready." Her "fine linen is the righteous deeds of the saints" (19:7-8). The marriage supper of the Lamb is celebrated as a result of Christ's death and resurrection; but, Christians benefit from that victory only if they are willing to follow Christ unto the end in a hostile world. Their profession and their confession are the marks of their identity as Bride of the Lamb.

Here on earth the church is in her time of betrothal. In Bible times, the interim between betrothal and marriage was considered a time of preparation for the consummation and a time in which they were obligated to faithfulness. By analogy, the church, betrothed to the Lamb, now prepares and awaits the Lord's return in glory so that the eternal marriage feast may commence.

John is not saying that the heavenly banquet has begun. Rather, he points proleptically to the period of perfect peace and bliss that comes at the end of the millennium. He projects the future blessedness much in the same way as he had pointed to Babylon's fall (14:8) well before lamenting her actual fall in chapter 17 and 18. Similarly, in later chapters, John gives a preview of the transcendent joy that awaits the faithful at the time of the *parousia*, or the second coming of Christ.

Some interpreters are surprised to see the Greek word for woman or wife in Rev. 19:7 (γυνη) instead of the usual word for bride (νυμφη). It seems that John is making a deliberate connection with the woman of chapter 12 by his repetition of γυνη in chapter 19. Finally, when the heavenly blessedness is described in much detail in Rev. 21, the usual word for bride is twice used (vv. 2, 9); and, in 21:9 "bride" and "woman" or "wife" are used synonymously. Clearly, it is the faithful woman, who will be the Bride of Christ also when she is translated into glory.

The bride and the invited guests for the marriage supper (19:7, 9) are the same people. The term "woman" or "bride" is used collectively for all the people of God. To speak of both the bride and the invited guests in this way is typical of the style of apocalypse. Similarly, the bride is referred to also as the holy city and New Jerusalem in 21:2, 9-10. Earlier Scriptures had spoken of a great feast. Thus, Isaiah 25:6-8 described a banquet on Mt. Zion where the Lord swallows up death forever and wipes away all tears. 3 Enoch 48:10 also places this banquet in Jerusalem. In Luke 13:29, Jesus says that His people will come from all points of the compass to sit at table in God's kingdom. The blessedness of those invited is a word spoken with authority. John adds his voice to that of Scripture when he declares, "these are true words of God" (19:10). The suffering church needs to know that her tribulation will end when the Lamb returns at the end of the interval of preparation. For the church, the second coming will be a new and glorious beginning, not a terrible ending!

A Jewish wedding is described as consisting of four parts (Hendricksen, 215-216). The betrothal is followed by an interval of preparation. After that, the bride adorns herself and the groom comes for her to lead her in procession to the wedding feast. The feast includes the marriage supper, and usually lasted 7 days. John draws on this analogy in Rev. 19:7-9. He describes the betrothal of the church to Christ as reality. Already the time of preparation by the Lamb is complete. He has paid the dowry for His bride. With His blood He bought her; for her life He died. The bride who has cleansed her deeds in His blood is clothed with fine linen, bright and pure. She is declared righteous as God's act of grace. In the end, the Bridegroom will come for His bride (see Matt. 25). The ensuing feast will last not one week or two, but forever. Not surprisingly, the book closes with the repeated prayer of the church to the Bridegroom, "Come!"

Clearly the time of preparation is of critical importance. Matthew's parables stress this particularly. In the parable of the marriage of the King's son (Matt. 22:1-14), one of the guests failed to wear a wedding garment. Unlike the bride of Rev. 19:8, who clothed herself in fine linen (the righteous deeds of the saints), the man was ill-prepared, and was excluded from the feast. Isaiah 61:10 had spoken of the garments of salvation, the robe of righteousness, befitting this occasion, which had been given him. Similarly, John saw "the holy city, New Jerusalem, coming down out of heaven from God, prepared as a bride, adorned for her husband" (21:2).

Thus, the reader of sacred Scripture is urged to prepare for the coming of the Lamb. The garment of salvation is offered freely to all who would accept it. Wisely, 5 virgins of the Matt. 25 parable trimmed their lamps in readiness for the procession to the marriage feast. When the Bridegroom came, they entered the feast. The five foolish virgins who were unprepared for His coming found the door shut and themselves left to suffer the consequences.

As we carry the portraiture of the Bride into Rev. 21, we see John fusing this image with that of the holy city, New Jerusalem. The opposite picture is that of the fusion of the great harlot picture with that of Babylon. The church is where God is in the midst of His people. The Bride, the holy city, and New Jerusalem are all ways of portraying God's people and His intimacy with them. In the New Jerusalem, revealed after the millennium, the church is taken out of her evil environs and comes into completed blessedness. Certainly, John would tell his church that they are an alternative to secular society already in the present time as they look for the Lord's return. Being distinctive from the world is prerequisite to being properly adorned for the Lamb's high feast.

When John describes New Jerusalem as a bride adorned for her husband, he draws on common contemporary imagery. Rome itself had been portrayed as a woman, as the goddess Roma. The worship of her subjects was required for her. Polycarp's later martyrdom bears further testimony to that grim reality. John took strong exception to the worship of Roma and her personification, the emperor. He saw her as a spiritual prostitute. For John, the community of the faithful is represented by a very different woman. She is the bride who faithfully awaits the coming of the heavenly Bridegroom; and, she prays that His coming will be soon (22: 17, 20).

When the angel shows off the Bride as the Lamb's wife, the marriage is viewed as consummated (21:9). It is declared to be a done deal (21:6). The Bride is freely offered the water of life (compare John 4:13-14) and is given the heritage of being God's son (in another wonderful mixed metaphor, Rev. 21:6-7).

Amazingly, the invitation to view the Bride in 21:9 and the harlot in 17:1 is given in each case by one of the 7 angels who had the 7 bowls of the wrath of God. John seems to suggest that the appearance of the Lamb's Bride is related closely to the judgment of the great whore. One cannot live in both Babylon and New Jerusalem. Entry into the presence of God requires the denunciation of all that Babylon signifies. The renunciation of sin is prerequisite to entry into the city of God as a son of God, and as Bride of the Lamb.

THE HARLOT

Who is this woman that John features so prominently? Before identifying her clearly as Babylon, John says much about her character. He introduces her in the same manner as he does the bride who enjoys the blessedness of New Jerusalem. Both women are shown forth by one of the 7 angels who had the 7 bowls. Different from the blessed Bride, the woman of Babylon is marked for judgment. John lists a multitude of her **evil characteristics**. They will be presented serially.

1. *Great harlot.* In Rev. 17:1 Rome is portrayed in the same way that Nineveh and Tyre had been described in the Old Testament. Nahum 3 described Nineveh as a city that inflicts her whoredoms upon the nations. Similarly, Isaiah 23:16-17 pictures Tyre as a forgotten harlot. Even Jerusalem is depicted as a harlot by the prophets (Isa. 1:21; Ezek. 16:15). Jeremiah 51 offers many other details about Babylon which John incorporates in his portrait of the great harlot (Murphy, 350-351). Opposite to the meritorious Bride, Babylon is utterly meretricious. Her glamor conceals her hostility to God, as she aggressively seduces people from their true allegiance. Her path is strewn with the allurements of idolatry and comely deceptions. Babylon stands for an imperial system that used seduction for possible personal gain from a persecuted minority.

2. *Seated upon many waters.* Rev. 17:15 explains the many waters on which the harlot sits as "peoples, multitudes, nations, and tongues." That stresses Babylon's universal influence. The picture comes from Jer. 51:13, where ancient Babylon is described as situated "by many waters." Similarly, Isaiah 8:7-8 predicted Assyria's invasion of Israel as "the waters of the River, the king of Assyria," rising "over all its banks" and sweeping "on into Judah." The numerous canals of the city Babylon which channeled the waters of the great Euphrates to the adjacent areas symbolize for John the dominance and influence of Rome as the city "flowed forth" to all her subject Mediterranean territories.

3. *Fornication with kings and earthlings.* Rev. 17:2 characterizes the harlot as fornicating with kings and as intoxicating "the dwellers

on earth" with her charms. Earlier, in 14:8, the angel had proclaimed Babylon's fall because she had forced the nations to "drink the wine of her impure passion." The emphasis on kings (as is also projected in 10:11), signals the interest of the latter half of Revelation in the political system of kings who are subservient to a dominating emperor who imposed alien religion. That the kings are culpable through their collaboration with Rome is clear. Both the sixth seal (6:15-16) and the sixth bowl (16:12-16) indicate this through kings who either flee the coming wrath or help bring it on. The kings will ultimately be made to serve God's purposes (17:17). For the Lamb is King of kings and Lord of lords (19:16), and He will ride forth in triumph over them in the end.

4. *Wilderness based.* Here the wilderness is not presented as a place of divine protection and nourishment (as in 12:6, 14). Rather, it is one of the places which the harlot frequents in order to persecute the righteous "woman" who had fled there. The wilderness had been the site of temptation both in Israel's exodus wanderings and at the start of Jesus' public ministry. Where God's people go, the Tempter will stalk them. Fortunately, Israel became a people in the wilderness, and Jesus overcame Satan in another wilderness. The church would not be spared demonic visitations; she must maintain her vigil and her resolve.

5. *Sitting on a scarlet beast, arrayed in purple and scarlet.* The scarlet beast is identified with the one that rose from the sea (13:1). Like its master, the red dragon (12:3), it is a terrifying presence. Her colors allude to her royalty and her ostentatious display of wealth. These symbols of Rome's luxury were designed to seduce mankind into the ways of Rome. The gaudy garb of the whore contrasts sharply with the "fine linen, bright and pure," worn by the Lamb's Bride (19:8).

6. *Bedecked with gold and jewels.* The prostitute's gold, jewels, and pearls reflect both her wealth and her seduction. The gold cup she holds promises carnal gratification. However, its contents are "the impurities of her fornication" and abominations. Such abominations are despicable in the presence of God, and should not exist among His people. They resist and insult divine sovereignty.

130

7. *A name of mystery on her forehead.* Names signify the character of a person. Roman harlots regularly wore their names on headbands in the public brothels. This trait, applied to Rome, further identifies her as corrupter of the nations. In Revelation itself identifying names are found on the foreheads of both the followers of the Lamb (7:3; 9:4; 14:1; 22:4) and of the beast (13:16). The names they bore reflect their loyalty to the Lamb or to the beast, and put them into the opposite camps of the good and the evil.

A name of mystery is not necessarily a puzzle. While it is a code word unknown to the uninitiated, it is very obvious to the inner circle. The mystery here is that "Babylon" refers to Rome. The persecutors are ignorant of the symbolism; but, the Christians understood well that the whole story was about Rome. She is the "mother of harlots and of earth's abominations" (17:5), another way of saying that she is the chief among spiritual whoremongers and evil-doers.

The beast which the woman rode also has "blasphemous names" (v. 3). These names insult God. If the woman is Rome, the beast she rode is the Roman Empire. Both Rome and her emperors claimed divine names such as those belonging only to the true God. The emperor's title, "augustus," meant "revered." "Divus" means "divine"; "dominus" is the name of "the Lord." All of these titles are God's unique right. Some emperors took the title "Soter" (Savior), that belongs to Jesus Christ. Domitian wished to be called "Dominus et Deus" (Lord and God). Clearly, these are serious fractures of the commandment that requires unique respect for the One Lord and God.

8. *Drunk with blood.* Rome reveled in the slaughter of Christians much as a drunkard is addicted to alcohol. She vigorously persecuted God's people and delighted in the blood of the martyrs. This is amply illustrated in the Apocalypse by such vignettes as those related in 2:13, 6:9, 11:7-10, and 20:4. Sadly, one notes that the 20th century world was exceptionally "drunk with the blood" of the saints, and especially so in Europe, Asia and Africa, as has been widely documented.

The scarlet woman is closely allied with the beast. She sits upon it and participates in its program. Their agendas coincide. Thus, a few of the beast's characteristics pertain to the woman's sphere of operation also. Therefore, we list them here as well.

131

THE BEAST:

9. *"Was, is not, ascends from the pit, and will go to perdition"* (17:8). Rev. 20:1-3, 7-10 refers to the demise of Satan in the same way. The one who was temporarily shackled will reappear from the pit to bring on the end, through which he himself meets his dire fate. Rev. 17:8 presents the beast as a parody of God and the Lamb, Who "is, was, and is to come" (Rev. 1:4, 8; 4:8). The Nero *redivivus* myth is presented similarly in 13:3-4 in terms of the mortal wound that was healed. John distinguishes between God and "the beast" by noting that the latter will be destroyed. God will not be mocked. Finally, His truth and justice will prevail.

10. *"Has 7 heads which are 7 hills and 7 kings"* (17:9). Here the mystery is revealed. The Christians are given "wisdom" regarding the identity of the beast. Rome was built on 7 hills, a fact well known in antiquity. The number of the beast, 666, given in 13:18, also had called for wisdom. These two are the only citations in Revelation where wisdom is invoked. Six is the number of evil. The tripling of 6 emphasizes the immensity of the evil. Clearly, Rome, the harlot, and the beast are of the same cut of cloth. Of the 7 kings, who are the 7 heads, interestingly, the sixth king is the one who is "now" (17:10). Being "sixth" points to his depravity, symbolized by the numeral used. Most scholars agree that this is a reference to Emperor Domitian who sent John to exile and persecuted the church.

11. *"Will be conquered by 'the King of kings.'"* Under future kings, the empire will fall (17:10-11). The ten horns (symbolizing completeness of power) will be the agents for the empire's eventual demise. These agents of power, or kings, will be conquered by the Lamb against Whom they war. For the Lamb is "King of kings and Lord of lords" (17:13-14; 19:16). The attempt to connect the kings with names is a fruitless exercise. The symbolism of the Apocalypse, given to the numbers 6 (evil), 7 (perfection), and 10 (completeness), clearly carries the message of God's final victory over the forces of evil. The 10 kings (however many that is) will effect God's purposes in bringing down "the harlot Babylon" when the King of kings finally intervenes. Despite John's use of symbolic numbers, he makes a very

literal use of the number 7 in respect to the seven hills, which are universally recognized as being the location for Rome.

The King of kings will not be a solitary conqueror. He will be accompanied by those who are His own, those "called, chosen, and faithful" (17:14; 19:14). He will not abandon those who have followed Him. They are His by gracious adoption. They "are His retinue, not His resources" (Morris, 212). Such loyalty is not found between the beast and the harlot, as we examine yet another characteristic of the beast.

12. *"Will self-destruct."* Rev. 17:15-18 shows that there is disunity among the forces of evil. Their wickedness leads to jealousy and hatred. They will destroy each other. The fall of Babylon is lamented poetically and formally by monarchs, merchants, and mariners alike in Rev. 18. Conversely, the hosts of heaven sing forth their four-fold "Hallelujah" in chapter 19 as prelude to the Lamb's marriage to the Bride. The forces of evil having been put down, it is time to celebrate God's reward for the saints who faithfully endured.

A comparison of the harlot and the bride, as seen in their portrayals in Rev. 17-22 is given below in tabular form.

The harlot	The Bride
A bowl angel says, "Come, I will show you" (17:1)	A bowl angel says, "Come, I will show you" (21:9)
The judgment of the great harlot (17:1)	The marriage of the wife of the Lamb (19:7; 21:2, 9)
Fornicated with kings and earthlings (17:2)	Is clothed, bright and pure (19:8)
Seated among many waters (17:3)	Coming down out of heaven (21:10)
Full of blasphemous names (17:3)	Is "The holy city Jerusalem" (21:2, 9-10)
Wears purple, scarlet; gold, jewels, and pearls (17:4; 18:16-17)	Is radiant, like a rare jewel, jasper, crystal (21:11)
A name on her forehead (17:5)	God's name on foreheads (22:4)
Mother of abominations (17:5)	No abomination (21:27; 22:3)
Names not in the book of life (17:8)	Names in the book of life (21:27)
Seated on 7 hills (17:9)	Seen from a high hill, coming down from heaven (21:10)
Kings will destroy her (17:15-18)	Kings will bring their glory to her (21:24)
She will be naked (17:16)	She is clothed in fine linen (19:8)
The great earthly city (17:18)	The holy city, coming down from heaven (21:2, 9-10)

FOR STUDY AND REFLECTION ON:

THE BRIDE

1. Identify each of the dragon's 3 intended victims and describe the outcome of his attack.
   a. The child (Rev. 12:1-6)
   b. Michael (12:7-12)
   c. The woman (12:13-18)

2. Who do each of the above 4 characters represent?

3. Tell which of the 5 names given the dragon in Rev. 12:9 is most appropriate; and, briefly state what that name means to you.

4. The Gospels refer to confrontations between Jesus and Satan. Briefly describe the outcomes of the events of:
   a. Matt. 2:13-15 (see Rev. 12:4-5)
   b. Matt. 4:1-11
   c. Matt. 16:21-23
   d. John 13:21-30

5. From Rev. 12:11:
   a. List several ways the devil is overcome.
   b. Which of these can you identify with?

6. When the devil fails to destroy the anointed child (Jesus), whom does he pursue (12:13, 17)?

7. Give the background (from Exodus) for the protection of the woman (12:14, 16).

8. Compare the length of the time references in 12:6 and 12:14. How do these compare with the time of the church in the world?

9. How is the woman of Rev. 12 related to the Bride of 19:7?

10. Who are the ones invited to the Lamb's marriage supper? What does that say to the life of the church today?

11. How does the marriage supper of 19:9 differ from "the great supper of God" portrayed in 19:17-18, 21?

12. What is notable about the difference between the clothes of the Bride (19:8) and that of the harlot (17:4 and 18:16)? What spiritual message does that give?

13. Explain the relationship of the holy city, New Jerusalem, and the Bride (Rev. 21:2-4; 9-11). How does God's presence with His people factor into all of this?

14. Why would the Bride find the Lamb (21:9) to be a desirable husband? Give your response on the basis of the following references:
    a. Rev. 5:6-14;
    b. 7:13-17; and,
    c. 12:10-11.

THE HARLOT

1. What is the nature of the harlot's fornication? (Rev. 17:1-2)

2. Read Ezekiel 16 and 23 to answer the following.
    a. What is different from Rev. 17 about the harlotries (and the harlots) mentioned in Ezekiel?
    b. What is similar?

3. The scarlet beast (17:3-6).
    a. Compare it with the dragon of 12:3-6.
    b. Note their colors and their manner of doing violence to the book's "heroes."

4. Given the woman's "possessions," who do you think were her lovers (or benefactors)? [See 17:4; also, chapter 18 gives some hints.]

5. Compare the writing on the foreheads of the 144,000 (14:1) with the writing on the harlot's forehead (17:5).

6. Compare 13:1-3 and 17:7-8. Describe the relationship of the beasts referred to in the two places.

7. "A woman by any other name . . . ."
   a. Are the harlot (the woman "arrayed in *purple and scarlet*," 17:4) and the beast (17:7-9 and 18:16) the same "person"?
   b. Is the harlot a city (17:9, 18)?
   c. Account for the multi-ethnicity of the harlot's clients (17:9, 15; 18:9).

8. What can Christians expect if they compromise with the harlot Babylon (18:4-8)?

9. The harlot's destruction.
   a. List the various groups that praise God at the harlot's destruction (19:1, 4, 5)?
   b. Did the harlot go to hell (20:15; 21:8)?

10. Describe ways in which Christians can
    a. Be "in the world,"
    b. But not "of the world."

CHAPTER X

THE SURPRISING SEVEN "SEVENS"

Seven is John's favorite number. He uses it often and with great variety. Seven symbolizes the sum of things in heaven (represented by three) and on earth (denoted by four). It is the perfect number, and it often reflects totality. Revelation has fifty four occurrences of it. Seven spirits appear as seven torches before the throne and send greetings to the seven churches of Asia, which are depicted as seven lampstands. Their spiritual leaders are variously dubbed as seven stars or seven angels. The scroll of human destiny has seven seals, which can only be opened by the Lamb, Who has seven horns and seven eyes. Seven angels blow seven trumpets; again, seven angels have seven plagues and pour out seven bowls of wrath. Seven thunders sound private revelations to John. A great earthquake kills seven thousand when the two witnesses go up to heaven. Seven heads top the dragon, the beast from the sea, and Babylon's scarlet beast, showing their kinship. Seven diadems rest on the red dragon. Seven hills and seven kings identify Babylon. In addition, there are other series of seven which are not numbered, e.g., seven signs, sights, beatitudes, attributes of praise, and the concluding word of appeal, "come." John's sevens serve as vehicles for his message as well as means by which he shows the progression of revelation.

SERIES OF SEVENS

Perhaps the dominant use of the number seven in Revelation is in the several significant series. The seven letters seem to initiate a series of sevens that give some sort of structure to the Apocalypse. In reality, however, another sequence of seven has already been initiated before the seven letters, as I will show later.

For most readers, however, the structure of the book seems somewhat amorphous and more than a little confusing, if not overwhelming. Most readers will quickly spot three other sequences of sevens (seals, trumpets, and bowls) as they wend their way through the rugged terrain of the book. Even many scholars are content to stay with these four clearly numbered sevens as the only significant series of sevens.

Not so for others who have sought to scale the peaks of the book's formidable structure and content! Thus, William Heidt (<u>The Book of the Apocalypse</u>) posited two added sevens in the latter half of the book–seven **signs** and seven **sights**. In my attempt to discover the criterion used by Heidt for his assertion, I discovered, with only very small shifts in Heidt's division points that the key was the introductory verb ειδον, "I saw." This morpheme not only opens each section of the seven signs that precede the seven **bowls**; but ειδον also dominates the opening verse of each of the seven **sights** which follow the seven bowls.

Heidt's terminal points for the later seven sights, however, left some challenges, but seemingly surmountable ones. However, having later examined Austin Farrer's work, <u>A Rebirth of Images: The Making of St. John's Apocalypse</u>, a somewhat altered pattern from what Farrer saw came through with utter clarity, also based on the recurrent verb form, ειδον. Farrer's terminal points ran from Rev. 19:11-21:8 (as compared to Heidt's seven sights seen in 18:1-20:15). The opening signal, using ειδον, came through with remarkable consistency in Farrer's scheme. Also the clustering by numbers of visions and the climactic progressions within these two new sevens proved consistent with the pattern of the more obvious numbered sevens elsewhere in Revelation. When I later discovered that Frederick Murphy's <u>Fallen is Babylon: The Revelation to John</u> followed Farrer's division points, my strong hunch turned into firm conviction. Having been thus persuaded by my own primary studies, and building on recognized scholarship, I offer the following three propositions.

First, a simplified outline for Revelation is advanced, based on the several series of sevens, thus giving structure to what some see as an amorphous collection of visions. Then, a renewed focus is given to two recognized series of unnumbered "sevens," on the basis of formal and material considerations, as carriers of the message. Finally, the

Seven Beatitudes are presented as a seventh significant series of "seven," an eschatological overlay accentuating the apocalyptic hope of the faithful as they endure present tribulations.

The seven beatitudes, sprinkled from end to end of the book, draw the message together through an indispensable gospel vehicle that must not be overlooked. This is especially true if one hopes to see the book as more than a series of messages of trials, tribulations, and terminations. "Blessed, blessed, blessed," John repeats over and over as a seven-fold eschatological hope for the faithful! Because of the beatitudes, the followers of the Lamb that was slain find joy and hope at every turn after the accounts of their own suffering or after the flattening of the oppressive persecutors by the divine sledge hammer of judgment. Some modern videos and other casual interpretations on the Apocalypse miss the joy it promises and presents: namely, the revelation of the redemption brought by the Lion of the tribe of Judah. This is perhaps due in part to their failure to distinguish between those who are "the tribes of the earth" (i.e., the persecuting imperial and other false religionists) and the followers of the Lamb. Nevertheless, John consistently brings hope for the redeemed after citing the evils that befall mankind, including Christians, during the earthly sojourn. More on the beatitudes later!

SEVENS SHAPE THE STRUCTURE

First, then, let us look at the outline of Revelation, based on its formal structures while mindful also of its meaningful and dynamic content.

I. Introduction
    A. Prologue and Introductory Greeting (1:1-8)
    B. Christological vision (1:9-20)
    C. The *Letters* to the Seven Churches (2:1-3:22)
II. Divine Providence Revealed
    A. Vision of the Glory of God and of the Lamb (4:1-5:14)
    B. The Seven *Seals*, with two penult interlude visions (6:1-8:5)
III. The Seven *Trumpets*, with two penult interlude visions (8:6-11:19)
IV. The Seven *Signs* (12:1-15:4)

V. The Judgment of the Wicked
   A. The Seven *Bowls* (15:5-16:21)
   B. The Babylon Appendix (17:1-19:10)
VI. Conclusion
   A. The Seven *Sights*(19:11-21:8)
   B. The New Jerusalem Appendix (21:9-22:5)
   C. Epilogue (22:6-21)
VII. The Seven *Beatitudes* (1:3; 14:13; 16:15; 19:9; 20:6; 22:7; 22:14)

Series of sevens provide the pattern for the Apocalypse. The seven **beatitudes** are introduced in the prologue and are completed in the epilogue. In between, John presents series of seven **letters, seals, trumpets, signs, bowls, and sights.** Each plays its role. The opening letters to the seven churches are general messages for the whole church, duly credentialed by the divine visions that precede and follow. The seven seals reveal the life of the church in the world amid the struggles of time and place, but as providentially sealed and secured. The seven trumpets that follow cover similar ground, but with heightened intensity and detail. Repetition underscores the realities of life in the world.

As Revelation enters its second half, seven **signs** depict the conflict between Satan and the Lamb, as vivid pictures describe the Lamb's victory and the coming judgment. The focus of the seven **bowls** then briefly and swiftly concentrates judgment on the terrestrial and celestial opponents of the people of God and the Lamb. The climax of the book comes in the seven **sights**. They reveal the decisive defeat and judgment of all evil foes as well as the magnificent reward and eternal life of the faithful redeemed. Fittingly, Revelation's closing prayer can only be, "Amen, come Lord Jesus!"

THE PATTERN OF THE TWO UNNUMBERED SEVENS

The first half of Revelation seems to move with relative ease from the seven letters to the seven seals and the seven trumpets. However, once the reader moves past chapter 11, and commences on the last 11 chapters of the book , there is only one numbered seven left–that of the seven bowls; and, it is buffered on both sides by sections of similar length that seem amorphous and confusing to the casual reader. Permit me, then, to present an outline, first for the seven signs, and later for the seven sights that flank the seven bowls of the wrath of God. For each of the two sections I offer observations about both formal and material aspects of the message.

THE SEVEN SIGNS (12:1-15:4)

1. The **dragon** pursues: (12:1-17)
   a. the child (vv.1-6)
      v. 1, "And a great **sign** *was seen* in heaven, a woman . . . "
      v. 3, "And another **sign** *was seen* in heaven, note well: a great red dragon"
   b. Michael (vv. 7-12)
   c. the woman (vv. 13-17)
2. A **beast** rose from the **sea** (13:1-10);
      v. 1, "And *I saw* a beast . . . ."
3. A **beast** rose from the **land** (vv. 11-18);
      v.11, "And *I saw* another beast . . . ."
4. The **Lamb** stood on Mt. Zion (14:1-5);
      v. 1, "And *I saw*, note well: the Lamb"
5. Three **angelic** proclamations (vv. 6-13);
      v. 6, "And *I saw* another angel . . . ."
6. "One like a Son of Man," and three **angelic** reapers (vv. 14-20);
      v. 14, "And *I saw*, note well: a white cloud . . . ."
7. **The Song** of Moses and the Lamb **before the seven angels** (15:1-4).
      v. 1, "And *I saw* another **sign** in heaven...seven angels...."
      v. 2, "And *I saw* what appeared to be a sea of glass...."

In each of the visions of "the signs" the defining mark is the introductory verb ειδον, "I saw," in place of which ωφθη, "there was seen," found twice near the start of the first vision, is an acceptable equivalent.[1]

In both the opening and closing visions of the seven "signs" the word σημειον, sign, is used---twice in the opening vision, once in the closing one. The signs point to the opponents in the struggle: the woman, representing God's people; the Satanic dragon; and, the seven angels. The angels in the seventh vision signal the final conquest of evil and the victory celebration of the redeemed. Interestingly, the beast from the sea (which looks like a lamb) also does signs; but, as 13:13-14 testifies, it can do them only as permitted. The point is that the Satanic agent has its limits, and must stop short whenever the Almighty "reins in the tether."

Also notable is the use of the imperative form of the same key verb, ιδου, found in three striking locations in these seven visions. In 12:3 it is used to signal the presence of the great red **dragon**: in 14:1 it reveals the **Lamb** in the midst of the 144,000 on Mt. Zion; and, in 14:14 it points to the white **cloud** which bears one like a **Son of Man**. These are the principals in the struggles of human destiny. The dragon is the antagonist; the Lamb and the heavenly figure seated on a cloud portray the protagonist who reaps the vintage (where the dragon and his retinue are trodden underfoot). "Note well," ιδου, the writer says, this struggle is the ultimate showdown, and it involves the primary forces of good and evil.

AN INTERIOR PATTERN

As is true with the seven seals, trumpets, and bowls, so also the first four of the "seven signs" have a strong bond. The dragon and the two beasts form an "unholy trinity" in the first three visions to oppose the Lamb, Who dominates the fourth vision. The dragon's three swings, successively at the Incarnate One, at Michael and his angels, and then at the one who bore the child, net a decisive "strike-out" (12:1-17). The two beasts, as the second and third members of the dragon's team, then go to bat against the faithful. Although they inflict considerable damage, the game is far from over. For the Lamb is more than equal to the threat (14:1-5). The aftermath of the struggle finds Him in a victory celebration on Mt. Zion, surrounded by those who received the crown of life. Interestingly, the third of the "unholy trinity" (dragon, beast, and false prophet) is a false lamb, with two horns, practicing its deceits in the vision preceding that of the true Lamb's celebration on Mt. Zion.

The final three visions of the seven signs pertain to angels, the supporting cast of the Lamb. As in the visions of the seals, trumpets, and bowls, here there is also a pairing of the fifth and sixth visions, followed by a climactic seventh. In the fifth vision (14:6-13) there are three angelic announcements of the coming judgment, from which, of course, the faithful departed are spared (v. 13).[2] The immediately following sixth vision dramatically depicts the reaping of the harvest, culminating in the treading of the winepress of the wrath of God against His adversaries (14:14-20). The closing vision of the seven signs shows the celebration of the conquering saints who sing the Song of Moses and the Lamb in the presence of the seven angels.

Thus, the second half of the book opens with seven unnumbered visions, carrying the main story line of the book, the triumph of good over evil and the vindication and reward of the saints; this happens both in the great judgment of those whose names are not in the book of life and in the blessedness "henceforth" of those who have been faithful unto death.

The series opened with the birth of the child (the Advent or our Lord) in 12:1-5, and closed with references to the Second Coming when Jesus, the Son of Man, returns on the cloud of heaven (see Daniel 7) in judgment. The time frame between these two comings of Jesus is the same as the 42 months, or the 1260 days, and the 3½ days, and the "time, times, and a half" of chapters 11 and 12. Perhaps amazingly, the reader will discover, it also equals the 1,000 years of chapter 20, at the end of which time the judgment happens before the "great white throne." It remains for the sixth series of sevens (which follows the seven numbered bowls) to bring this victory over "the unholy three" to its dramatic, glorious, and fitting consummation.

The visions of the seven signs also include, at 14:13, the first beatitude since Rev. 1:3. It gives a foretaste of the joys to come to those who endure the ravages of time. More on that later in the section on the beatitudes!

THE SEVEN SIGHTS (19:11-21:8)

Before commenting on the seven sights, a few transitional words about the seven bowls are in order. The outpouring of the seven bowls of God's wrath is the connecting link between the seven signs and the seven sights, and it targets specifically "the men who bore the mark of the beast" (16:2). The reference to Babylon (first mentioned in 14:8) now comes into sharp relief (in 16:19), and moves on to a full-blown appendix (17:1-19:10), graphically depicting the demise of Babylon, the visible and present, but fading, villain of the Apocalypse. This section on the bowls and Babylon is the longest one of the book, suggesting that the judgment of the evil is more than a footnote in history, or an idea that can easily be brushed aside as a non-event. God's judgment on the evil is as serious as His salvation of the righteous is glorious!

Next, the writer advances to the climax of the book as he presents the wondrous consummation found in "the seven sights" (19:11-21:8) with its awesome appendix on the New Jerusalem (21:9-22:5). The seven sights are also, without exception, formally introduced by the morpheme ειδον. They are as follows.[3]

1. The **Victorious Horseman**, Faithful and True (19:11-16)
    v. 11, "Then *I saw* heaven opened, and note well, a white horse!"
2. **An Angel** summons the birds to feast on those slain (19:17-18)
    v. 17, "Then *I saw* an angel standing in the sun . . . . "
3. The **Beast and** the **False Prophet** are thrown into the lake of fire (19:19-21)
    v. 19, "And *I saw* the beast and the kings of the earth ...."
4. The **Binding of Satan** (20:1-3)
    v. 1, "Then *I saw* an angel coming down from heaven ...."
5. The **1,000 year reign** of the blessed; then, Satan in the **lake of fire** (20:4-10).
    v. 4, "Then *I saw* **thrones**, and seated on them . . . . "
6. The **final judgment** before the great white throne (20:11-15)
    v. 11, "Then *I saw* the great white **throne** . . . . "
    v. 12, "And *I saw* the dead ... standing before the **throne**"
7. The **New Jerusalem** comes down out of heaven (21:1-8)

> v. 1, "Then *I saw* a **new** heaven and a **new** earth . . . . "
> v. 2, "And *I saw* the holy city, **New** Jerusalem . . . . "
> ["Note well" occurs also in vv. 3 and 5.]

Again, in the "seven sights," as in the "seven signs," the defining mark is the introductory verb ειδον, found in each opening line of the particular "sight." In the "seven signs" the ειδον verb was found twice in the opening and closing visions. Similarly, for the "seven sights," the same verb (ειδον) is doubled in two visions, the last two, as if to bring closure to the series of the sevens found in a consecutive format in the Apocalypse. Probably of even greater moment for the reader is the climactic nature of the message. The faithful are now given a vision of their blessedness in God's own presence, a vision that will explode into glorious magnificence in the appendix on New Jerusalem that follows (21:9-22:5).

As was true for the "seven *signs*," so the imperative, ιδου, (of the same verb ‘οραω), is found thrice in pivotal locations in the "seven *sights*." In the opening verse of the first "sight," the ιδου ("behold" or "note well!") heightens attention to the white horse and its rider who rides forth victoriously in behalf of those who were worthy of His name, "Faithful and True" (19:11). Later, ιδου causes the reader to "note well" two great truths which make all the difference for those who will see the New Jerusalem. First, the visionary announces, "**Behold**, the dwelling of God is with men . . . , and they shall be His people" (21:3). Then, as if to reassure the reader, He adds, "**Behold**, I make all things new . . . . These words are trustworthy and true" (21:5). The reader can hardly miss the tie-in of the next statement, "*It is done!*" (21:6). It brings vivid reminder of the significance of the completed work of the Lamb Who was slain, Whose victory cry on Calvary was, "*It is finished!*" (John 19:30). The victory of Good Friday initiated the later revelation of heaven's fullness of glory yet to come.

As was true with the earlier "sevens," the seven sights also show a tight bond between the first four in the series. Then, they continue with a tandem, followed by a climactic conclusion. After the first four visions of the final and decisive showdown, there follow two throne visions and a final vision of the new heaven and the new earth. In sequence, the seven sights depict the conquering heavenly armies; the earthly opponents; the confinement of the beast and the false prophet; followed by the binding of Satan "for a 1,000 years." The fifth and sixth sight reveal successively the *enthronement* of the faithful who would reign with Christ "for 1,000 years," and the judgment scene before the One who sat on "the great white *throne*." The grand climax of sights is that of the joyous presence in the New Jerusalem of those who "shall be His people, and God Himself will be with them" (21:3).

Additionally, Farrer has pointed out (Rebirth, p. 57) that the first four visions show a vertically downward progression from above. The battle moves down from the heavenly armies to the earthly battle scene; then follows the disposal of the two beasts into the fiery lake and the imprisonment of the Devil to the depths of the bottomless pit.

Perhaps it is not too much of a stretch to add that the vertical direction of the saints, as reflected in the final three sights, goes in the opposite direction. The fifth sight reveals not only the faithful martyrs' participation in the first resurrection, but also their enthronement. Next, they are gathered with all others before the great throne to be lifted up by the happy verdict that they are included in the book of life which gives them clearance from the second death. Finally, of course, there is the translation to the holy city, which is portrayed as rising to a height of 12,000 stadia (21:16).

That city, the *New* Jerusalem, is God's *new* creation, truly a *new* heaven and a *new* earth. It is devoid of all the evils that plagued the fallen world and its fallen center, *Old* Jerusalem, and its corrupted temple (as well as the perverse "Babylon" and all that it represents). That *new* city is the *new* home to which God's saints happily aspire. It has and needs no rebuilt replica of the *old* temple "for its temple is the Lord God the Almighty and the Lamb" (21:22).

The "seven sights" are not without a beatitude. Rev. 20:6 signals the blessedness of those who share the "first resurrection" (who thus avoid the doom of the "second death"). They will "reign" with Christ the symbolic 1,000 years as they await the final blessedness depicted in the beatitudes of the epilogue (22:7, 14). The triumph of the faithful was long in coming. However, both the plaintiff cry of the faithful martyrs, "How long?" (6:10), and the hopeful expectation of the reader of the Apocalypse are finally and richly rewarded. Those who faithfully endure to the end will find their blessedness (1:3; and, 22:7). That blessedness is stated in transcendent language, as the limitations of human experience allow the reader only to imagine what the vision of the New Jerusalem presents as real.

THE BEATITUDES OF THE APOCALYPSE

There is a paucity of comment on the beatitudes of the Apocalypse in the religious periodical literature. A survey of Religion Index One: Periodicals (from 1977-2008) revealed not a single treatment of this theme there. Even so, I would list John's seven statements of beatitude and reflect on their role in advancing the purpose and message of the book. They are as follows:

1. "Blessed is he who reads aloud the words of the prophecy, and blessed are those who hear, and who keep what is written therein; for the time is near." (Rev. 1:3)
2. "Blessed are the dead who die in the Lord henceforth. Blessed indeed," says the Spirit, "that they may rest from their labors, for their deeds follow them!" Rev. 14:13)
3. "Blessed is he who is awake, keeping his garments that he may not go naked and be seen exposed!" (Rev. 16:15)
4. "Blessed are those who are invited to the marriage supper of the Lamb." (Rev. 19:9)
5. "Blessed and holy is he who shares in the first resurrection." (Rev. 20:6)
6. "Blessed is he who keeps the word of the prophecy of this book." (Rev.22:7)
7. "Blessed are those who wash their robes, that they may have the right to the tree of life and that they may enter the city by the gates." (Rev. 22:14)

John's purpose is clearly one of giving hope to God's oppressed saints. It is as though the beatitudes echo the message of the Apocalypse as a commentary on the words of Jesus, found in John's Gospel. "I have said this to you that in Me you may have peace. In the world you have tribulation; but be of good cheer, I have overcome the world." (John 16:33)

The seven beatitudes are interspersed from end to end of Revelation to remind the reader that he who is faithful unto death receives the crown of life (2:10). Since the perfect number seven is clearly John's number of choice, it is no surprise that he gives us exactly seven beatitudes. (Thus he differs from Matthew, who has nine; and, from Luke, who has four "blesseds," followed by four matching "woes"; and, both evangelists offer them in a consecutive block of teaching.)

With the exception of the one beatitude found in the prologue, all of John's beatitudes are in the second half of the book. Between the first two there is a long interlude of nearly fourteen chapters. That pattern is totally reversed from the seven seals and the seven trumpets; there lengthy interludes separate the last two of the series. It is as though John allows the reality factor of persecution and tribulation to be recycled a few times before repeatedly uttering the healing words of blessing.

Different from the **woes** in Matthew and Luke, which are spoken against the outsiders of the faith, the woes that John depicts lacerate even the believers in their daily walk. These woes originate with the dragon and his henchmen. These woes can and will be overcome as the faithful keep their focus on the Lamb Who was slain and has ransomed men for God (5:9). These woes are not fully ended until the dragon who was thrown down from heaven (12:9), and later thrown into the bottomless pit (20:3), is finally thrown into the lake of fire and brimstone to be tormented forever (20:10). Then, and only then, is the third woe finally at an end!

Having turned aside from the woes first inflicted by the evil foe and his followers, and then consummated upon the erstwhile afflicters with boomerang force, let us turn back to the beatitudes.

The primary focus of the beatitudes, as also of the whole Apocalypse, is eschatological. Different from the general genre of apocalyptic literature, the tone has a vibrant air of optimism and hope about it. Indeed, there is the sense of realism that we live in an imperfect world, and that it will get worse before it gets better. But, there is the difference! It will get better! Nay, it will become the best! So excellent, in fact, that words cannot convey the fullness of the content of blessedness.

In keeping with the concept that witness is borne by two or three (Deut. 19:15; Gen. 41:32), the beatitudes proceed in two's or three's to bear testimony to the virtue and blessedness of fidelity. Beatitudes *One and Six* (found in the opening and closing chapters) trumpet the benefit of keeping the words of this book. Both do so with an eye to eschatology. Beatitude One ends with the reminder that "the time is near." Reason enough to read, hear, and keep these words! Beatitude Six comes immediately after the promise, "Behold, I am coming soon"; again, reason enough to pay heed!

Similarly, Beatitudes *Two and Five* (Rev. 14:13 and 20:6) share common content. The blessedness of the souls of those who die in the Lord is that they will reign with Him the "1,000 years" preceding the Lord's return. "They may rest from their labors" (14:13). They have eternal life as through their belief in Jesus they have "passed from death to life"(John 5:24). Thus, they have the blessedness of the "first resurrection." The "second death" (separation from God) will have no power over them (Rev. 20:6).

Beatitudes *Three, Four, and Seven* (Rev. 16:15; 19:9; and, 22:14) all have to do with being properly *dressed* for "the great day of God"(16:14). The one who is awake and keeps his *garments,* avoiding nakedness at "Armageddon," is "blessed" (16:15-16). "Those who wash their *robes* may enter the heavenly city and benefit from the tree of life (22:14). They are the bride of the Lamb and were "*clothed with fine linen,*" bright and pure (19:8). Those so garbed are truly blessed to be "invited to the marriage supper of the Lamb" (19:9).

The reader who keeps the promises of the seven Beatitudes firmly in mind has much to look forward to. Such "reading, hearing, and keeping the words of prophecy" will empower him to be faithful unto death. For the crown of life certainly is worth it!

---

[1]The reader will observe that the two cited verb forms are both derived from ‘οραω. The former is the first singular aorist active form of this irregular verb, while the latter is the third singular aorist passive of the same verb.

[2]It is at 14:13, the beatitude of those who die in the Lord, that I find myself in disagreement with Heidt regarding the division point between the fifth and sixth vision. Heidt has v. 13 start the sixth vision even though it has no ειδον in the verse. My issue with him is on two grounds. First, formally, the ειδον or its equivalent signals the start of all the other visions of "the seven signs." On the basis of content also, I prefer v. 13 to serve as a powerful consolation for the saints in the immediate context of the dire judgment of those bearing the mark of the beast. It is an uplifting "call for endurance." Thus, it shows a huge progression over the earlier "call for endurance" in 13:10 (in keeping with the thematic progression of the book.) The first "call," in effect, simply reassures that *evil* is a real part of our *earthly* life, so "persevere!" That is small comfort! By way of contrast, the call for endurance in 14:13 gives a glimpse of the *blessedness* of the life of *the world to come.* Happily, Farrer (Rebirth) agrees with my division points.

[3]The message of the seven sights is couched in an impressive chiastic pattern. The first and last of the sights focus on the glorious victory of the followers of "the Lamb." Sights two and six focus on the universal judgment at the end. Sights three and five each include mention of the lake of fire as the destiny of God's opponents. The central focus is on the assurance that man's mortal enemy, Satan, has been subdued and shackled. These sights can be structured as follows.

A (1) Heaven is opened (Note well!) [19:11-16]
   B (2) The finality of the universal judgment [19:17-18]
      C (3) The lake of fire (for the beast and false prophet) [19:19-21]
         D (4) Satan is bound [20:1-3]
      C' (5) The lake of fire (for Satan) [20:4-10]
   B' (6) The finality of the universal judgment [20:11-15]
A' (7) Heaven is opened (Note well!) [21:1-8]

BIBLIOGRAPHY

"A Lutheran Response to the Left Behind Series." A Report of the C.T.C.R. of the LCMS. St. Louis, 2004.

Barclay, William. Letters to the Seven Churches. Philadelphia: The Westminster Press, 1957.

-----. The Revelation of John. 2 vols. The Daily Study Bible Series. Philadelphia: Westminster, 1959.

Beasley-Murray, G. R. The Book of Revelation. New Century Bible Commentary. Grand Rapids: William B. Eerdmans Publishing Company, 1981.

Becker, Siegbert W. Revelation: The Distant Triumph Song. Milwaukee: Northwestern Publishing House, 1985.

Bible, Holy. Revised Standard Version.

Blake, Edward C. & Anna G. Edmonds. Biblical Sites in Turkey. Published in Pergamum, 1977.

Brighton, Louis A. Revelation. Concordia Commentary. St. Louis: Concordia Publishing House, 1999.

Dawn, Marva. Joy in Our Weakness: A Gift of Hope from the Book of Revelation. St. Louis: Concordia, 1994.

Farrer, Austin. A Rebirth of Images: The Making of St. John's Apocalypse. Albany: S.U.N.Y. Press, 1986.

Franzmann, Martin H. The Revelation to John. St. Louis: Concordia, 1976.

Goldsworthy, Graeme. The Lamb & the Lion--The Gospel in Revelation. Nashville: Thomas Nelson Publishers, 1984.

Heidt, William. The Book of the Apocalypse. N. T. Reading Guide. Collegeville, MN: The Liturgical Press, 1962.

Hemer, Colin J. The Letters to the Seven Churches of Asia. The Biblical Resource Series. Grand Rapids: Eerdmans, 2001.

Hendriksen, William. More Than Conquerors. Grand Rapids: Baker Book House, 1967.

Hughes, Philip Edgcumbe. The Book of the Revelation. Grand Rapids: Eerdmans, 1990.

Jenkins, Ferrell. The O.T. in the Book of Revelation. Grand Rapids: Baker, 1972.

Kautz, Darrel P. Understanding the Book of Revelation. Milwaukee: Published by the author, 1985.

Krodel, Gerhard A. Revelation. Augsburg Commentary on the N.T. Minneapolis: Augsburg Publishing House, 1989.

Lindsey, Hal with C. C. Carlson. The Late Great Planet Earth. Grand Rapids: Zondervan Publishing House, 1970.

Love, Julian P. The Revelation to John. The Layman's Bible Commentary. Atlanta: John Knox Press, 1960.

Luther, Martin. Prefaces to the New Testament. Translated by Charles M. Jacobs. Revised by Theodore Bachmann. Reprint of Fortress Publication. St. Louis: Concordia, 1972.

Metzger, Bruce M. Breaking the Code. Nashville: Abingdon Press, 1993.

Morris, Leon. The Book of Revelation. Tyndale N.T. Commentaries. Revised edition. Grand Rapids: Eerdmans, 1987.

Mounce, Robert H. The Book of Revelation. The New International Commentary on the New Testament. Grand Rapids: Eerdmans, 1979.

-----. What Are We Waiting For? A Commentary on Revelation. Grand Rapids: Eerdmans, 1992.

Murphy, Frederick. Fallen is Babylon. Harrisburg, PA: Trinity Press International, 1998.

Onstad, Esther. Courage for Today, Hope for Tomorrow – A Study of the Revelation. Revised and expanded edition. Minneapolis: Augsburg, 1993.

Plueger, Aaron Luther. Things to Come for Planet Earth. St. Louis: Concordia, 1977.

Religion Index One.

Richardson, Donald W. The Revelation of Jesus Christ. Atlanta: John Knox Press, 1976.

Rist, M. "Apocalypticism," The Interpreter's Dictionary of the Bible. Vol. I. New York: Abingdon, 1962.

Roloff, Juergen. The Revelation of John. Translated by John Alsup. Minneapolis: Fortress Press, 1993.

Swete, Henry B. Commentary on Revelation. Grand Rapids: Kregel Publications, 1977.

-----. The Apocalypse of St. John. Third edition. Grand Rapids: Eerdmans, 1908.

Talbert, Charles H. The Apocalypse. Louisville: Westminster John Knox Press, 1994.

The "End" Times. A Study on Eschatology and Millennialism. A Report of the C.T.C.R. of the LCMS. St. Louis, 1989.

"The Martyrdom of the Holy Polycarp, Bishop of Smyrna," The Apostolic Fathers: An American Translation by Edgar J. Goodspeed. New York: Harper & Brothers, 1950.

CPSIA information can be obtained at www.ICGtesting.com
Printed in the USA
235616LV00001B/10/P